DECISION MAKING FOR FINITE MATHEMATICS

DALE BUSKE
St. Cloud State University

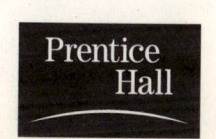

Prentice Hall

Upper Saddle River, NJ 07458

Editor in Chief: Sally Yagan
Acquisitions Editor: Quincy McDonald
Supplement Editor: Joanne Wendelken
Assistant Managing Editor, Math Media Production: John Matthews
Production Editor: Donna Crilly
Supplement Cover Manager: Paul Gourhan
Supplement Cover Designer: PM Workshop Inc.
Manufacturing Buyer: Ilene Kahn

Prentice Hall

© 2002 by Prentice Hall
Prentice-Hall, Inc.
Upper Saddle River, NJ 07458

All rights reserved. No part of this book may be reproduced in any form or by any means, without permission in writing from the publisher.

The author and publisher of this book have used their best efforts in preparing this book. These efforts include the development, research, and testing of the theories and programs to determine their effectiveness. The author and publisher make no warranty of any kind, expressed or implied, with regard to these programs or the documentation contained in this book. The author and publisher shall not be liable in any event for incidental or consequential damages in connection with, or arising out of, the furnishing, performance, or use of these programs.

Printed in the United States of America

10 9 8 7 6 5 4 3 2 1

ISBN 0-13-042883-3

Pearson Education Ltd., *London*
Pearson Education Australia Pty. Ltd., *Sydney*
Pearson Education Singapore, Pte. Ltd.
Pearson Education North Asia Ltd., *Hong Kong*
Pearson Education Canada, Inc., *Toronto*
Pearson Educacíon de Mexico, S.A. de C.V.
Pearson Education—Japan, *Tokyo*
Pearson Education Malaysia, Pte. Ltd.

Contents

Preface   vii

0 Spreadsheet Basics   1

1 Functions, Models and More   4
    1.1 Functions 4
       1.1.1 Building Weather Calculators 4
       1.1.2 Rent-A-Car 7
       1.1.3 Interest is Simple 9
    1.2 Linear Models 11
       1.2.1 Predicting the Consumer Price Index 11
       1.2.2 Modeling Wage Growth of Production Workers 15
       1.2.3 A Looming Health Insurance Crisis? 16
       1.2.4 Setting Ticket Prices 17
    1.3 Using Goal Seek 19
       1.3.1 Finding the Equilibrium Price 19
       1.3.2 Seeking Savings 23
       1.3.3 Do We Still Need Algebra? 25
    1.4 Appendix – Using the Chart Wizard 27

2 Matrices   30
    2.1 Adding Matrices 30
    2.2 Multiplying Matrices 32
    2.3 Computing Inverses 36
    2.4 Solving Linear Systems 41
       2.4.1 Computing Return on Investment by Catagory 42
       2.4.2 Planning a Daily Diet 43
       2.4.3 The Hilbert Matrix 44
    2.5 Gauss-Jordan Elimination 45
    2.6 The Transpose 47
    2.7 Determinants 49

CONTENTS

2.8	Leontief Input-Output Analysis	51

3 Linear Programming — 53
- 3.1 The McDonald's Diet 53
- 3.2 Petroleum Blending 58
- 3.3 Nonlinear Programming 63
- 3.4 Linear Least Squares 65
- 3.5 Portfolio Optimization: Markowitz's Quadratic Model ... 68
- 3.6 Appendix 72

4 The Simplex Method — 73
- 4.1 Finite Mathematics Tutoring 73
- 4.2 Curing Math Phobia 77
- 4.3 Feeding the Survivors 80
- 4.4 Bubble Head Dolls 83
- 4.5 Which Optimal Solution? 85
- 4.6 Cycling 89

5 The Mathematics of Finance — 91
- 5.1 Building Custom Financial Calculators 91
- 5.2 Making Decisions Using Financial Spreadsheet Calculators ... 95
  - 5.2.1 Offering a CD 95
  - 5.2.2 Buying a House 97
  - 5.2.3 Winning the Lottery 99
- 5.3 Amortization Schedules 101
- 5.4 IRA's 104

6 Probability Distributions — 107
- 6.1 The Binomial Distribution 107
- 6.2 The Negative Binomial Distribution 111
- 6.3 SuperLoserLotto 115
- 6.4 The Hypergeometric Distribution 119
- 6.5 The Normal Distribution 123
- 6.6 Approximating the Binomial Distribution 126

7 Descriptive Statistics — 129
- 7.1 Sorting Through It All 129
- 7.2 Frequency Distributions 131
- 7.3 Sizing up a Data Set 137
- 7.4 Measuring Spread 140
- 7.5 Some Theory 143

8 Game Theory — **145**
  8.1 Strictly Determined Games 145
  8.2 Rock, Scissors, Paper 148
  8.3 Let's Add Dynamite 150

9 Markov Chains — **155**
  9.1 S&P Bond Ratings 155
  9.2 Raising Neptunian Iguanas 158
  9.3 Tennis Anyone? 161
  9.4 Game, Set, Math! 163
  9.5 Tumblin' Gumballs 165
  9.6 Juvenile Recidivism in New South Wales 167
  9.7 Appendix 168

Index of Excel Commands — **169**

Preface

Though spreadsheets have been used for hundreds of years by accountants, only recently has the use of computerized spreadsheets been possible. It wasn't until 1978 that a computer program called *VisiCalc* (short for visual calculator) written by Harvard Business School student, Daniel Bricklin[1] emerged. *Visicalc* was the first "killer" application for personal computers. In fact, much of the early growth of the personal computer industry should be credited to the spreadsheet.

The dynamic powers of the modern spreadsheet have opened new doors to the learning process. These spreadsheets give a user the ability to easily change input data and have the spreadsheet *automatically* change any output from one or a series of calculations. Other attributes of the spreadsheet include the ability to allow the user to easily discover patterns in numerical data, to graphically display data, and to perform mathematical and logical operations with ease. Further, Microsoft *Excel* allows even novice users the ability to combine the powers of a programming language such as Visual Basic making for even greater flexibility than ever before.

Today's world is one in which spreadsheets are used in nearly every business. However, the purpose of this text is not just to provide students with a introduction to the use of spreadsheets. The purpose of this text is instead to *use* the modern spreadsheet as a *tool* for solving problems and *making decisions*. It is intended to help students better understand algorithms and formulas used in finite mathematics. One purpose in using the spreadsheet is to avoid messy arithmetic which may be involved in the search for patterns in data, in solving real-world problems, and/or in making decisions based on the output of an algorithm.

The use of the spreadsheet to "discover" mathematical ideas is ripe with possibilities. One aim of this text is to begin to exploit those possiblities. Another goal of the text is to put less emphasis on routine calculation and more emphasis on the decision process used in setting up a problem and in interpreting a solution.

The text is to be used as a companion to many finite mathematics textbooks such as those written by Armstrong and Davis, Barnett and Ziegler, or Goldstein, Schneider, and Siegel to mention but a few. The exercises serve as the major component to this text. *Do the exercises. Mathematics is not a spectator sport!*

---

[1] Check out his story at http://www.bricklin.com/

Chapter 0

Spreadsheet Basics

A spreadsheet is a rectangular grid of dynamic **cells** indexed by a column letter and a row number. We identify a particular cell in the second column and third row of the grid by using the notation B3. The spreadsheet in Figure 1 shows the conversion of several different lengths given in feet to meters.

	A	B
1	Feet	Meters
2	3	0.9144
3	1	0.3048
4	15	4.572
5	0.5	0.1524

Figure 1: Converting feet to meters with a spreadsheet.

The key behind effectively using spreadsheets is the use of **formulas**. Formulas allow a user to change input in one or more cells and have the *spreadsheet* automatically update output. Since 1 foot is approximately 0.3048 meters, we use the formula =A3*0.3048 in cell B2. If one wanted to repeat this process of conversion on the remaining three measurements given in feet, one would simply need to **copy** the formula in cell B2 to the cells B3 through B5 below it as shown in Figure 2. Notice that the formula changes when copied. When the formula from cell B2 is copied into cell B3, it becomes the formula =A3*0.3048. This is because the reference to cell A2 is a **relative cell reference**. If the user had used the **absolute cell reference** =$A$2*0.3048 when entering the formula in cell B2, the resulting number in cell B2 would be the same. However, if *this* formula would have been copied to cells B3 through B5 below, then all of the cells in column B would have given the same output 0.9144.

CHAPTER 0. SPREADSHEET BASICS   2

	A	B
1	Feet	Meters
2	3	=0.3048*A2
3	1	=0.3048*A3
4	15	=0.3048*A4
5	0.5	=0.3048*A5

Figure 2: Formulas used in converting feet to meters with a spreadsheet.

The idea behind a relative cell reference is that by using the formula =A2*0.3048, the computer is taking the value in the cell to its left, multiplying that value by 0.3048 and putting the resulting number in cell B2. Relative to the location of B2, the formula is getting its input from the cell that is in the same row but one cell to the left. This explains what happens when this formula is copied down column B to produce the output of Figure 1.

On the other hand, if the absolute cell reference =$A$2*0.3048 were used in cell B2, then the formula is getting its input from cell A2 period. That is, regardless of where this formula is copied, the input will continue to come from cell A2.

What would happen if another type of absolute cell reference were used in cell B2, say =$A2*0.3048? The output to cell B2 would remain the same as before; however, when the formula is copied down to cells B3 through B5 below, the new formulas are slightly different. The 'correct' output is still given, but cell B3 now contains the formula =$A3*0.3048. If *this* formula were copied over to cell C3, it would produce the same output as what is in cell B3. Note that this would not happen if a purely relative cell reference were used. The idea is that the formula is getting its input from the *same row* and from column A, not from the column to the immediate left.

To further illustrate this idea, consider what happens when the slightly different formula =A$2*0.3048 is used in cell B2. The output to cell B2 is again the same, however it is what happens when the formula is copied down column B that is interesting. The output in cells B3, B4, and B5 is the same as the output in cell B2. Why? The formula is getting its input from the absolute row 2 of the column to the left (in this case A).

Formulas in spreadsheets are always preceded by an equals (=) sign. Note also that mathematical operands such as +, -, *, /, and ^ are essentially the same as for a scientific calculator. For example, if we wanted to convert the measurements in column A from feet to yards, we would use the formula =A2/3 in cell B2. At this point, the reader should also note what happens when the input to cell A2 is changed. The output in column B is *automatically updated*. This is the power and beauty of modern dynamic spreadsheets.

Mathematical operations such as the summation of values from many cells can also be handled easily in a spreadsheet. To sum the values located in cells A2 through A5 and put the resulting sum in cell A7, we would type the formula =SUM(A2:A5) in cell A7. Note that we could also use the formulas =SUM(A$2:A$5) or =SUM($A$2:$A$5) to complete this task equally well. The difference in these two formulas is explained by copying this formula to cell B7. The first formula would copy to cell B7 as =SUM(B2:B5) and the second formula would copy as =SUM(B$2:B$5). The third fomula would copy to =SUM($A$2:$A$5) giving the same output as cell A7.

Chapter 1

Functions, Models and More

1.1 Functions

Understanding the concept of a function is of fundamental importance in using a spreadsheet effectively. In this section, we will gain a better understanding of how a function works by learning about how spreadsheets attempt to represent functions.

1.1.1 Building Weather Calculators

[Download: WeatherProject.xls]

On a trip to Brazil, Ian notes that temperatures are often listed in Celsius degrees rather than in Fahrenheit degrees. He would like to have a calculator which could instantly convert temperatures given in Celsius to temperatures in Fahrenheit. This is a simple task for a spreadsheet.

Before we can begin work on the spreadsheet, we need to understand how Celsius and Fahrenheit degrees are related to one another. A quick trip to the almanac (or internet!) returns the formula

$$F = \frac{9}{5}C + 32$$

where C represents the temperature in degrees Celsius and F represents the corresponding temperature in degrees Fahrenheit. In mathematical terms, we say that Fahrenheit temperature is a **linear function** of Celsius temperature.

Figure 1.1 illustrates a Celsius to Fahrenheit calculator built within the spreadsheet 'Celsius to Fahrenheit.' The construction of this calculator consists of putting the formula =9/5*A2+32 in cell C2. With this, the spreadsheet simply takes the Celsius value which the user inputs into cell A2, computes the corresponding Fahrenheit temperature according to the conversion formula, and outputs the resulting Fahrenheit temperature to cell C2.

CHAPTER 1. FUNCTIONS, MODELS AND MORE

	A	B	C
1	Celsius Temperature		Fahrenheit Temperature
2	-10		14.0

Figure 1.1: A Celsius to Fahrenheit calculator.

The important part of this calculator is that it is *dynamic*. That is, as soon as a user decides to change the input in cell A2 to a different value (a new Celsius temperature), the output cell (Fahrenheit temperature) is *automatically updated*! Would you like to know what 25 degrees Celsius is represented as in degrees Fahrenheit? Simply type 25 in cell A2. As you progress through this text, you will more fully appreciate the power of dynamic spreadsheets.

Formulas within spreadsheets can have more than one variable input. To illustrate this, we will develop a 'heat index calculator.' For temperatures over 70 degrees Fahrenheit, the heat index can be found using the complicated looking formula[1]

$$\begin{aligned} HI = & -42.38 + 2.049T + 10.14H \\ & -0.2248TH - 0.006838T^2 - .05482H^2 \\ & +0.001229T^2H + 0.0008528TH^2 - 0.00000199T^2H^2 \end{aligned}$$

where T represents the temperature in degrees Fahrenheit, H represents the relative humidity as a percentage, and HI represents the heat index. The spreadsheet 'Heat Index' within the workbook `WeatherProject.xls` illustrates how this calculator works. The key formula,

```
=-42.38 + 2.049*A2 + 10.14*C2 - 0.2248*A2*C2 - 0.006838*A2^2 -
    0.05482*C2^2 + 0.001229*A2^2*C2 + 0.0008528*A2*C2^2 -
             0.00000199*A2^2*C2^2
```

appears in cell E2.

	A	B	C	D	E
1	Temperature (F)		Relative Humidity		Heat Index
2	90		70		105.5289

Figure 1.2: A Heat Index calculator.

1. Imagine that the Rio De Janeiro weather forecast is for 35 degrees Celsius when Ian is scheduled to arrive on a trip. Use the calculator in the 'Celsius

---
[1]Source: National Weather Service

CHAPTER 1. FUNCTIONS, MODELS AND MORE 6

to Fahrenheit' spreadsheet of the workbook `WeatherProject.xls` to decide whether he should wear shorts and a T-shirt or a light jacket on the plane.

2. Just for fun, Ian would like to convert degrees Celsius to degrees Kelvin. He knows the formula which does this is

$$K = C + 273$$

where C is the temperature in degrees Celsius and K is the corresponding temperature in degrees Kelvin. Alter the formula in the 'Celsius to Fahrenheit' spreadsheet to change the calculator accordingly.

3. Those who live in the northern plains of the U.S. have grown accustomed to a measure called the **wind chill factor**. The wind chill factor is computed according to the formula

$$WC = 0.0817(3.71\sqrt{V} + 5.81 - 0.25V)(T - 91.4) + 91.4$$

where V represents the wind speed in MPH, T represents the temperature in Fahrenheit, and WC represents the corresponding wind chill factor.

Use the 'Wind Chill Factor' spreadsheet in the workbook `WeatherProject.xls` to finish the development of a 'wind chill factor calculator' by entering an appropriate formula in cell E2.

Note: To enter a square root such as $\sqrt{7}$ into a spreadsheet, we type `=SQRT(7)`.

> **You make the call:** Laura is traveling to the United States from Brazil and is accustomed to hearing temperatures given in Celsius degrees. Upon landing in Minneapolis, it is predicted that the temperature will be -35 degrees Fahrenheit. Build a dynamic 'Fahrenheit to Celsius' spreadsheet so as to help Laura decide whether she should wear a light or heavy jacket to Minnesota.

CHAPTER 1. FUNCTIONS, MODELS AND MORE   7

1.1.2 Rent-A-Car

[Download: CarRentalProject.xls]

For spring break, Geddy wishes to rent a car for 7 days to drive from Chicago to somewhere in the southern United States. Hurtz Rent-A-Car offers a 7-day rental for $250 plus 10 cents a mile. Avus Rent-A-Car offers a 7-day rental for $175 plus 15 cents a mile.

Let us suppose that Geddy wanted to drive 2700 miles (round trip) to Ft. Lauderdale, Florida. Then the cost of renting from Hurtz would be $250+(2700)(.10)=$520 and the cost of renting from Avus would be $175+(2700)(.15)=$580. Obviously, Geddy would rent from Hurtz in this case.

Since Geddy doesn't know exactly where he wants to go, but guesses that he will probably travel between 1000 and 2000 miles during the 7 days, he would like to look at several scenarios to help him decide with whom to reserve a car. The spreadsheet shown in Figure 1.3 shows some of Geddy's calculations.

	A	B	C
1	Miles	Hurtz Cost	Avus Cost
2			
3	1000	350	325
4	1100	360	340
5	1200	370	355
6	1300	380	370
7	1400	390	385
8	1500	400	400
9	1600	410	415
10	1700	420	430
11	1800	430	445
12	1900	440	460
13	2000	450	475

Figure 1.3: Calculations used in the car rental problem.

To construct the spreadsheet shown in Figure 1.3, Geddy started by putting 1000 in cell A3. He then placed the formula =A3+100 in cell A4 and copied it down column A until he reached 2000 miles in cell A13. Once column A was generated, Geddy went to work on columns B and C. In cell B3, Geddy used the formula =250+A3*0.10. The spreadsheet then outputs the amount Hurtz would charge for a trip having the length given in the cell to the left. By copying this formula down column B, Geddy was able to compute costs for various trip lengths between 1000 and 2000 miles. After copying, notice how cell B6, for example, contains the formula =250+A6*0.10.

CHAPTER 1. FUNCTIONS, MODELS AND MORE   8

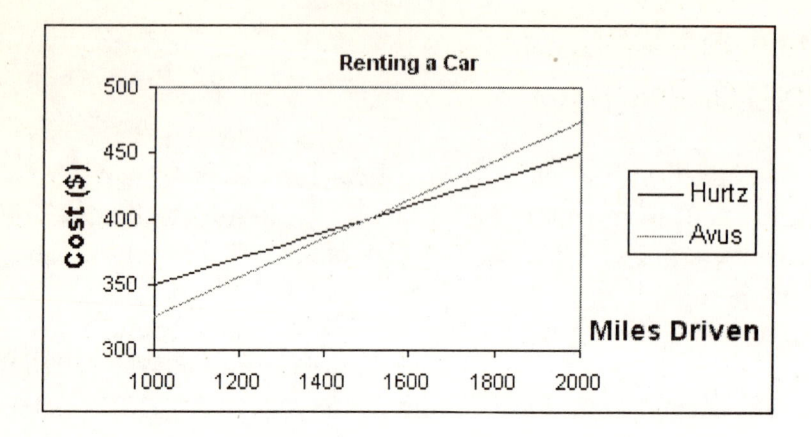

Figure 1.4: A graph using Geddy's calculations.

1. How is it that Geddy constructed the values in column C of Figure 1.3?

2. Based on Geddy's output, which car rental company should he rent from if he wants to drive from Chicago to Dallas (1850 miles round trip) for spring break? What if he plans on spending break in Nashville (935 miles round trip)? Can you modify the spreadsheet 'Car Rental Project' accordingly?

3. Suppose that Geddy would like to consider yet another car rental company, American Car Rental, which is offering a special deal of $50 for a 7-day rental plus 25 cents per mile. Modify column D in the spreadsheet accordingly. Should Geddy consider using American for a 1,850 mile trip to Dallas?

4. Three linear functions have been used in this project. Identify each of them and compute the slopes and y-intercepts of each.

You make the call: Using the spreadsheet 'Car Rental Project' you have modified, fill in the remainder of the chart shown in Figure 1.5 for Geddy.

Company	Rent from if trip is between			
Hurtz		and		miles
Avus	362.5	and		miles
American	0	and	362.5	miles

Figure 1.5: Information Geddy can use to make a decision on a car rental company.

1.1.3 Interest is Simple

[Download: SimpleProject.xls]

Calculating simple interest is simple for a spreadsheet. Imagine loaning P dollars to your sister at an annual simple interest rate of r. The amount A owed to you after t years is given by the formula
$$A = P + Prt.$$

Figure 1.6 illustrates a simple interest calculator at work in the spreadsheet 'Simple Interest Calculator.' The key formula

$$\text{=A2+A2*A5*A8}$$

is located in cell C2. This calculator is *dynamic* in the sense that as soon as a user changes any of the values in cells A2, A4, or A6, the output is automatically updated.

	A	B	C
1	Principal P		Amount A owed
2	$100.00		$110.00
3	Rate R		
4	4.00%		
5	Time t (years)		
6	2.5		

Figure 1.6: A simple interest calculator.

The spreadsheet 'Simple Interest Over Time' as shown in Figure 1.7 plots the growth of principal P at an annual simple interest rate r as a function of time t. How is this done? We begin by placing the values of P and r in cells A2 and A4 respectively. Then, in cell A6, we place the value of 0. For the sake of illustration, suppose we want to plot the output over 2 year time intervals. Because of this, cell A7 contains the formula =A6+2. By copying the formula in this cell into cells A8 through A16, we recursively create a column of time t values 0,2,4,6,8,10,12,14,16,18, and 20.

In cell B6, we place the simple interest formula

$$\text{=\$A\$2+\$A\$2*\$A\$4*A6}$$

using a mix (Why?) of relative and absolute cell references. After copying this formula into cells B7 through B16 (note how the elements of the formula change), we have data we can plot. We simply need to press the plot graph button provided.[2]

---

[2] To learn how to plot data in Excel, see the Appendix at the end of chapter 1.

CHAPTER 1. FUNCTIONS, MODELS AND MORE

Figure 1.7 shows the results of this process. Notice how the output appears to be linear.

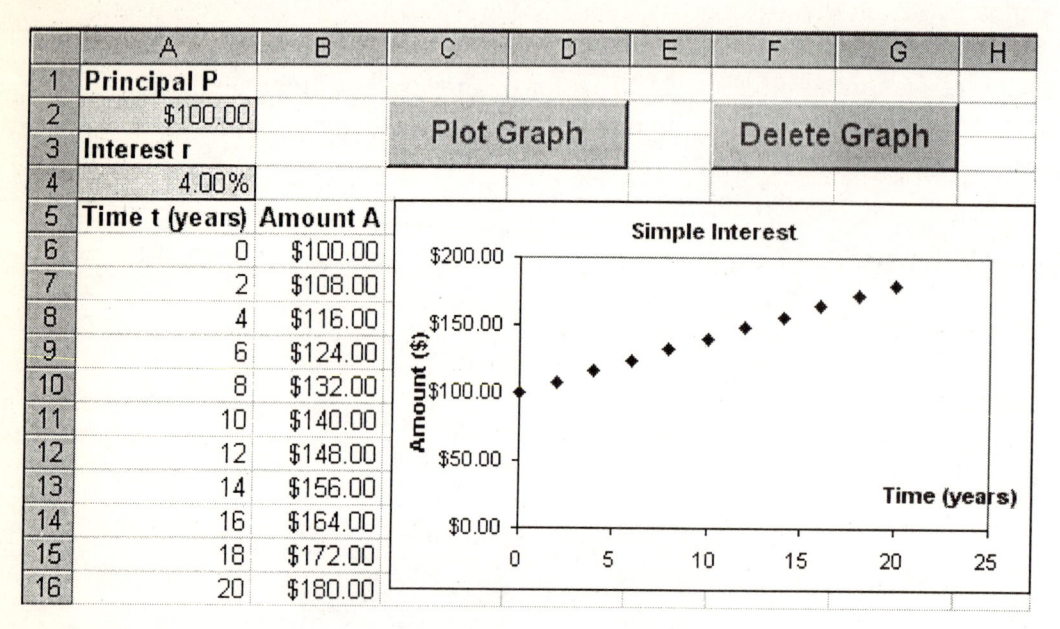

	A	B
1	Principal P	
2	$100.00	
3	Interest r	
4	4.00%	
5	Time t (years)	Amount A
6	0	$100.00
7	2	$108.00
8	4	$116.00
9	6	$124.00
10	8	$132.00
11	10	$140.00
12	12	$148.00
13	14	$156.00
14	16	$164.00
15	18	$172.00
16	20	$180.00

Figure 1.7: Plotting simple interest.

1. By making changes in the value of t, use the simple interest calculator in the spreadsheet 'Simple Interest Calculator' to estimate how many years (to the nearest tenth of a year) it will take for the amount of a loan of $1,000 to grow to $2,000 at an annual simple interest rate of 7%.

2. By making changes in the value of r, use the simple interest calculator in the spreadsheet 'Simple Interest Calculator' to estimate what annual simple interest rate (to the nearest hundredth of a percent) is needed in order for a loan of $1,000 to grow to $1,750 in 10 years. Does common sense tell you this is a reasonable answer?

3. Use the spreadsheet 'Simple Interest Over Time' to plot how an investment of $10,000 grows at 6% annual simple interest over the course of 15 years using one year intervals. Does the picture have the same shape as that in Figure 1.7? Should it? Explain.

> **You make the call:** How is simple interest affected by the annual simple interest rate r? Plot how an investment of $1 grows at various annual simple interest rates r over the course of 10 years using one year intervals. What do these graphs have in common? Can you draw any conclusions about the slopes of the lines being plotted?

CHAPTER 1. FUNCTIONS, MODELS AND MORE 11

1.2 Linear Models

Regression analysis is the process of fitting a function to a set of data points. Even though *Excel* can fit different types of functions to data, we will restrict our attention to **linear regression** – fitting data with linear functions. Of course, not all data is linear, but there are enough examples where data is approximately linear to warrant a brief look at linear regression.[3]

1.2.1 Predicting the Consumer Price Index

[Download: CPIProject.xls]

Consider the problem of finding a linear model for a given set of data (see Figure 1.8) representing the value of the Consumer Price Index (CPI) for the years 1987 to 1996.[4]

	A	B
1	Year	CPI
2	1987	113.6
3	1988	118.3
4	1989	124
5	1990	130.7
6	1991	136.2
7	1992	140.3
8	1993	144.5
9	1994	148.2
10	1995	152.4
11	1996	156.9

Figure 1.8: Consumer Price Index (CPI) for the years 1987 to 1996.

We begin by letting x represent the number of years since 1987 and $f(x)$ represent the value of the CPI. Because of our choice of x, we create a new column D containing the values of this variable. To generate these values, we place the formula =A2-1987 in cell D2 and copy this formula down column D. To retain the look of ordered pairs in our data, we will copy the values of column B into column E using cut and paste commands. The spreadsheet now appears as in Figure 1.9.

---

[3] A more indepth study of linear regression would require methods of calculus.
[4] Source: Bureau of Labor Statistics

CHAPTER 1. FUNCTIONS, MODELS AND MORE   12

	A	B	C	D	E
1	Year	CPI		Years since 1987	CPI
2	1987	113.6		0	113.6
3	1988	118.3		1	118.3
4	1989	124		2	124
5	1990	130.7		3	130.7
6	1991	136.2		4	136.2
7	1992	140.3		5	140.3
8	1993	144.5		6	144.5
9	1994	148.2		7	148.2
10	1995	152.4		8	152.4
11	1996	156.9		9	156.9

Figure 1.9: Modifying the CPI data.

Figure 1.10 shows a plot of columns D and E using a Scatter plot.[5]

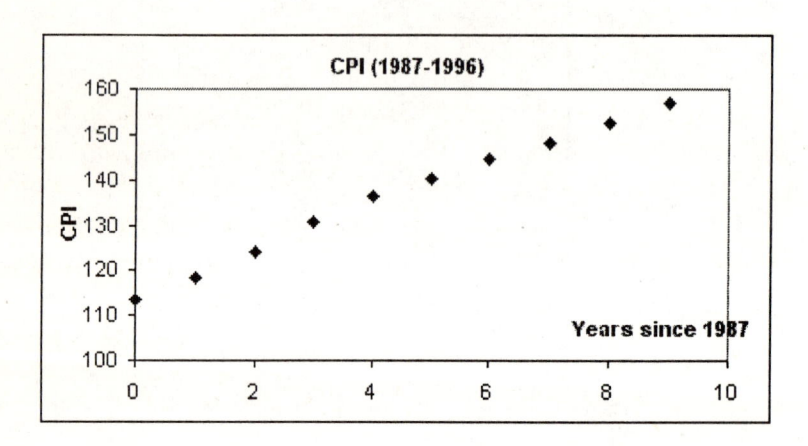

Figure 1.10: A scatter plot of the CPI data.

It is at this point that we find a linear model for the CPI data. Begin by highlighting (by clicking on) the scatter plot just created. Under the Chart menu in *Excel*, choose Add Trendline. In the Add Trendline menu, choose the Linear type and under the Options tab, select the two boxes labeled Display equation on chart and Display R-squared value on chart. *Excel* will find the best linear fit (using the least-squares method[6]) to the data plotted in the chart, will output and plot the line which best fits the data, and will output a number called the **coefficient**

---
[5]See the Appendix to chapter 1.
[6]See section 3.4

CHAPTER 1. FUNCTIONS, MODELS AND MORE

of determination. Output from this process applied to the CPI data appears in Figure 1.11.

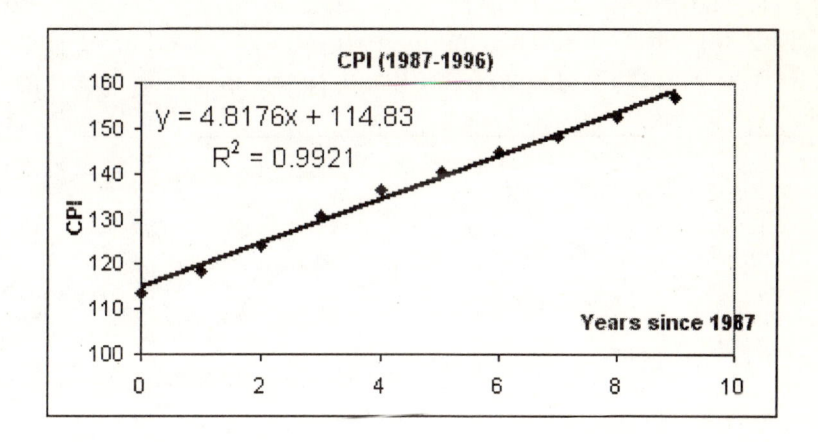

Figure 1.11: Finding a linear model for the CPI data.

What does the output that *Excel* gives mean? If x represents years from 1987 and $f(x)$ represents the value of the CPI, then the spreadsheet is telling us that $f(x) = 4.8176x + 114.83$ can be used as a model for the CPI. The R^2 value of 0.9921 tells us how well the function $f(x)$ fits the data. As a general rule, the closer this number is to 1, the better the function fits. A combination of the graphical output and the R^2 value suggests that the CPI can be modeled rather well by this function.

1. Use the output of Figure 1.11 to compute $f(10)$ and interpret its meaning.

2. The actual CPI index for 1997 was 160.5. How well did the model constructed in 'CPI Data' predict this outcome?

3. The CPI index for years 1997-2000 is shown in Figure 1.12. Use the information in the workbook `CPIProject.xls` and the regression capabilities of *Excel* to determine a linear model of the form $f(x) = mx + b$ for the 1987-2000 data. Use this model to predict the value of the CPI index for the year 2001.

Year	CPI
1997	160.5
1998	163
1999	166.6
2000	172.2

Figure 1.12: CPI data for years 1997-2000.

> **You make the call:** Data for the CPI index for 1913-2000 is given in the spreadsheet 'CPI Data 1913-2000.' Use the regression capabilities of *Excel* to determine a linear model of the form $f(x) = mx + b$ for the 1913-2000 data. Use this model to predict the value of the CPI index for the year 2001. Do you think this linear model is appropriate? Discuss.

1.2.2 Modeling Wage Growth of Production Workers

[Download: ProductionWageProject.xls]

Data representing the average hourly earnings of production workers in the U.S. can be found in `ProductionWageProject.xls`. Let x represent the number of years since 1964 and $f(x)$ represent the average hourly earnings of a U.S. production worker x years after 1964.

1. Use the regression capabilities of *Excel* to determine a linear model of the form $f(x) = mx + b$ for the given data.

2. In negotiations with the current union at the production company you work at, it is thought that wages will follow the U.S. average. Predict the average hourly earnings you should expect to be paying in the year 2010 according to the model found by *Excel*.

3. Was the actual average wage in 1984 above or below what your model predicts?

4. What does the model predict the average hourly wage of production workers in 1955 was? Do you think there are any limitations to this model? Explain.

5. Looking at the data, it appears that wages increase by a certain constant amount c each year. Estimate the value of this constant c. Does c appear to have anything to do with your linear model $f(x) = mx + b$?

> **You make the call:** Your father tells you that when he worked in production in the 1970's, wage increases were not what employees expected. Use the graphical results of the linear regression computed above to decide if your father's comment seems reasonable.

CHAPTER 1. FUNCTIONS, MODELS AND MORE   16

1.2.3 A Looming Health Insurance Crisis?

[Download: HealthInsuranceProject.xls]

Data representing the percent of Americans covered by health insurance in the U.S. can be found in `HealthInsuranceProject.xls`.[7] Let x represent the number of years since 1987 and $f(x)$ represent the percent of Americans covered by health insurance x years after 1987.

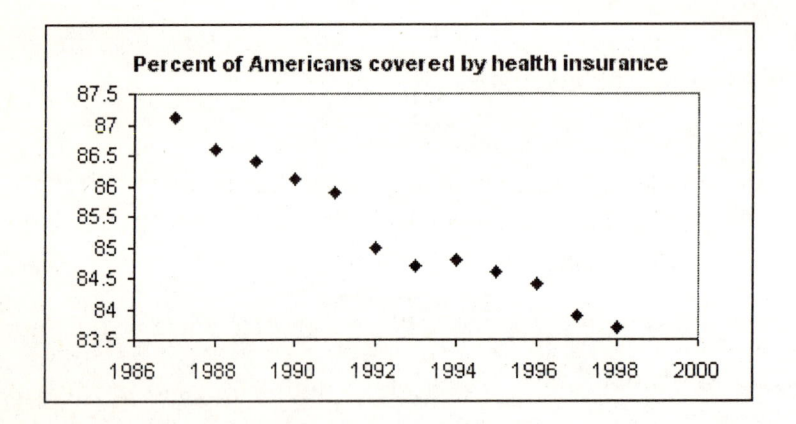

Figure 1.13: Percent of Americans covered by health insurance (1987-1998).

1. Use the regression capabilities of *Excel* to determine a linear model of the form $f(x) = mx + b$ for the data.

2. Predict the percentage of Americans that will be covered by health insurance in the year 2010 according to the model found by *Excel*.

3. What does the model predict the percentage of Americans covered by health insurance in 1944 was? Do you think there are any limitations to this model? Explain.

4. Looking at the data, it appears that the percentage of Americans covered by health insurance decreases by a constant c each year. Estimate the value of this constant c. Does c appear to have anything to do with the slope m of your linear model?

> **You make the call:** The 2000 U.S. census puts the American population at 281,421,906. What does your model say about the number of people *not* having health insurance in the year 2000?

---
[7]Source: www.census.gov

CHAPTER 1. FUNCTIONS, MODELS AND MORE 17

1.2.4 Setting Ticket Prices

[Download: OptimalRockProject.xls]

While many factors are involved in setting ticket prices for rock concerts, many times the prices are driven by demand and the desire of the performers to make money. In this project, we consider a fictional band of ex-finite mathematics students called 'Optimal Rock.' Optimal Rock has done some market research (experimentation!) and found price-demand data (see Figure 1.14) for their services.

Ticket Price	Demand
$25.00	100000
$35.00	80000
$40.00	70000
$50.00	45000
$75.00	20000
$100.00	1000

Figure 1.14: Price-demand data for Optimal Rock.

1. Use the regression capabilities of *Excel* to show that the best linear model for a price-demand function is

$$p(x) = -0.0007x + 92.582$$

where $p(x)$ is the price per ticket at which x tickets can be sold. Explain why it is logical that the slope of this line is negative.

2. The amount of revenue $R(x)$ that Optimal Rock can generate by selling x tickets is given by

$$R(x) = xp(x).$$

Fill in the spreadsheet 'Revenue Chart.' *Hint:* Begin by placing a formula in cell B2.

3. Plot a graph of the data you have just computed in the spreadsheet 'Revenue Chart.' Use a graph of this data to estimate the number of tickets Optimal Rock should sell in order to maximize their revenue.

You make the call: Optimal Rock has costs associated with each concert it produces. It costs $1,000,000 per concert plus $1.50 per audience member. Hence, the cost of putting on a concert for x fans is $C(x) = 1,000,000 + 1.5x$. Fill in the *Excel* spreadsheet 'Profit Chart' in the workbook OptimalRockProject.xls and use a plot of this information to estimate the number of tickets Optimal Rock should sell in order to maximize their profit $R(x) - C(x)$.

CHAPTER 1. FUNCTIONS, MODELS AND MORE   19

1.3 Using Goal Seek

There are times when we would like to ask the question "What input will give me this particular desired output?" For example, "How many widgets should we make to achieve a profit of $100?" or "If $y = 3x + 4$ and I want $y = 6$, what value should x be?" *Excel's* built-in Goal Seek command can help us determine answers to questions such as these.

1.3.1 Finding the Equilibrium Price

[Download: EquilibriumProject.xls]

We have all heard about the law of supply and demand. In fact, we live it everyday. This project will show how we can use *Excel's* Goal Seek command to determine the equilibrium (selling) price of tickets to FiniteFest – an annual gathering of those celebrating the beauty and utility of finite mathematics.

	A	B	C	D	E
1	Demand	Price		Supply	Price
2	900	$14.00		1500	$14.00
3	1100	$13.00		1350	$13.00
4	1300	$12.00		1200	$12.00
5	1500	$11.00		1050	$11.00
6	1700	$10.00		900	$10.00
7	1900	$9.00		750	$9.00

Figure 1.15: Price-demand and price-supply data for FiniteFest.

To start, we must realize both supply and demand for FiniteFest tickets are a function of the price of the tickets. Through some research, we can determine price-demand data and price-supply data as shown in Figure 1.15.

It is useful to plot this data on one chart[8] as shown in Figure 1.16. We can then use the linear regression capabilities of *Excel* to find that the demand curve can be modeled by

$$d(t) = -0.005t + 18.5$$

where t is the number of tickets that are in demand at a price of $d(t)$. Similarly, we find the supply curve can be modeled by

$$s(t) = 0.0067t + 4$$

---
[8]See the Appendix at the end of chapter 1 on how to plot data in *Excel*.

CHAPTER 1. FUNCTIONS, MODELS AND MORE   20

where t is the number of tickets that can be supplied at a price of $s(t)$.

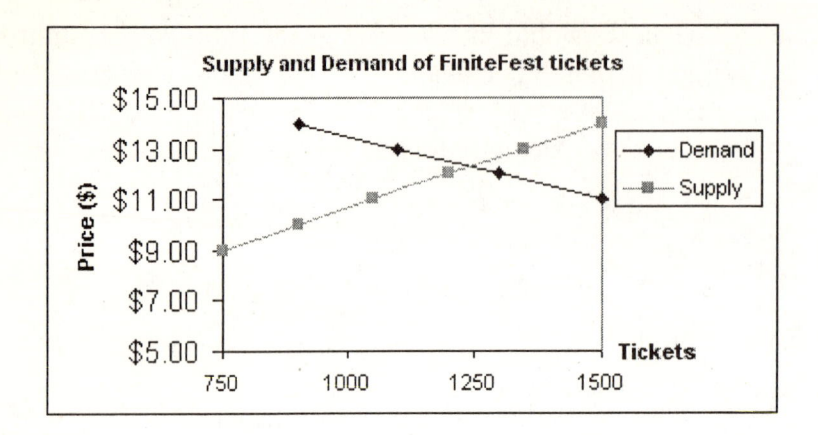

Figure 1.16: Plot of price-demand and price-supply data for FiniteFest.

Basic economics tells us that the equilibrium price will be set by the intersection of the supply and demand curves as shown in Figure 1.16. To find how many tickets will be sold, we want to determine the value of t such that $d(t) = s(t)$. To do this, we set up a chart as shown in Figure 1.17.

G	H	I	J	K	L
Tickets t		d(t)	s(t)		d(t)-s(t)
1000		13.5	10.7		2.8

Figure 1.17: Determining the selling price of FiniteFest tickets using `Goal Seek`.

In cell G2, we put our best estimate as to how many tickets we expect to sell at equilibrium. In cell I2, we place the demand formula =-0.005*G2+18.5. Similarly, in cell J2, we place the supply formula =0.0067*G2+4. In another cell, say cell L2, we compute the difference of these values with the formula I2-J2. Notice that we *want* this value to be zero! That is the *goal we seek*. To find the number of tickets t that will satisfy this goal, highlight cell L2 and choose `Goal Seek` under the menu item `Tools`.

CHAPTER 1. FUNCTIONS, MODELS AND MORE

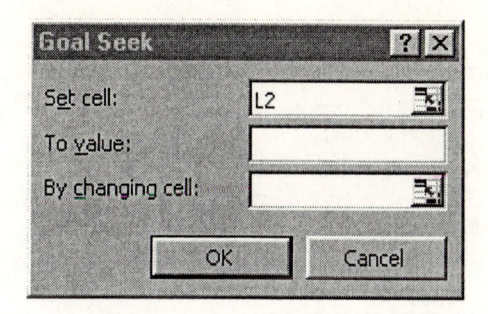

Figure 1.18: The Goal Seek prompt.

In Goal Seek, we set cell L2 (that is what we want to be 0) to the value of 0 by changing the values in cell G2. When Goal Seek runs, it returns values of approximately $12.30 to cells I2 and J2. This value is the equilibrium price at which FiniteFest tickets will be sold. In cell G2, we also find that approximately 1240 tickets will be sold at this price. Note that these values seem to match the location of the intersection point we found in Figure 1.16.

1. In setting the price of FiniteFest tickets, does it seem to matter what the initial value in cell G2 is set at when using Goal Seek?

2. How much ticket revenue will the coordinators of FiniteFest collect at the equilibrium price?

3. In an effort to enhance the finite mathematics knowledge in the U.S., suppose the government were to subsidize the cost of admission to FiniteFest by $2.00 for every individual who wanted to attend. That is, suppose new price-demand data looked like that shown in Figure 1.19.

Demand	Price
900	$16.00
1100	$15.00
1300	$14.00
1500	$13.00
1700	$12.00
1900	$11.00

Figure 1.19: Changing the demand curve for FiniteFest.

Use *Excel's* Goal Seek tool and regression capabilities to determine the new equilibrium price of FiniteFest tickets and approximate the number that will be sold.

You make the call: Consider the price-demand and price-supply data for FiniteFest II contained in the spreadsheet 'FiniteFest II' and shown in Figure 1.20.

Demand	Price	Supply	Price
900	$14.00	1500	$14.00
1100	$11.50	1350	$12.00
1300	$9.50	1200	$10.25
1500	$7.50	1050	$9.00
1700	$6.25	900	$7.50
1900	$5.25	750	$6.50

Figure 1.20: Data for FiniteFest II.

Fit an **exponential trendline** of the form Ae^{bt} to both the price-demand and price-supply data. Then, use *Excel's* `Goal Seek` tool to determine the new equilibrium price of FiniteFest tickets and approximate the number that will be sold.

CHAPTER 1. FUNCTIONS, MODELS AND MORE 23

1.3.2 Seeking Savings

[Download: SeekingSavingsProject.xls]

Sally would like to save some money for a popular finite mathematics text which costs $149.95. Sally currently has $A_0 = \$100.00$ that she is placing in a savings account which credits her interest annually at a rate of $r = 4.25\%$. Even without taking a finite mathematics course, Sally knows that after N years of compound interest, she will have

$$A_N = A_0(1+r)^N$$

dollars in her savings account. Sally wants to know how many years N it will take before she can reach her goal of saving $149.95.

Using the spreadsheet 'Annually Compounded Savings' and the `Goal Seek` tool in *Excel*, we can answer Sally's question. Figure 1.21 illustrates how we place the value of the initial amount A_0 in cell **A2** and the interest rate r in cell **A4**. In cell **A6**, we will simply place an estimate for the number of years N we believe it will take to reach Sally's goal. Lastly, to solve the problem, we place the compound interest formula `=A2*(1+A4)^A6` in cell **A8** and use the `Goal Seek` tool. In `Goal Seek`, we set cell **A8** to a value of $149.95 by changing cell **A6**. Output will be as in Figure 1.21. Sally needs to wait approximately 9.73 years before she can buy her book!

	A
1	Initial amount in savings account
2	$100.00
3	Interest rate r
4	4.25%
5	Number of years passed N
6	9.73365586
7	Amount in account after N years
8	$149.95

Figure 1.21: Solving Sally's savings problem using `Goal Seek`.

1. Suppose Sally found her finite mathematics book on sale for $129.95 at an online retailer. Use `Goal Seek` to determine how many years it would take before she had saved enough to buy the book.

2. Suppose that Sally is only willing to wait 2 years to buy the $129.95 book. Use `Goal Seek` to determine the interest rate her savings account will need to pay her to accomplish this task. *Hint:* Set the value in cell **A6** to 2 and allow cell **A4** to change during `Goal Seek`.

3. Quincy would like to buy a $29.95 CD-rom, but he has a different savings technique. Quincy initially has $4.85 in his piggy bank (earning no interest!) and adds $1.25 per week from his allowance. Use the spreadsheet 'Piggy Bank' and `Goal Seek` to determine how long Quincy has to wait to buy the CD-rom. *Hint:* You will need to put a (different) formula in cell `A8` before you `Goal Seek`.

4. Meisha is saving to buy a sporty new red Porshe costing $80,000.00. She is investing a lump sum of $65,000.00 in a savings account in which the interest is compounded quarterly at an annual rate of $r = 7.25\%$. Meisha knows that the compound interest formula is given by

$$A_N = A_0 \left(1 + \frac{r}{k}\right)^{kN}$$

where A_0 is the initial investment, A_N is the value of the investment after N years at an annual interest rate of r compounded k times a year.

Use the spreadsheet 'Compound Interest Savings' and `Goal Seek` to determine how long Meisha will have to wait before buying her Porshe.

5. How long will Meisha have to wait to buy her Porshe if the interest is compounded monthly?

6. How long will Meisha have to wait to buy her Porshe if the interest is compounded daily?

7. How long will Meisha have to wait to buy her Porshe if the interest is compounded hourly? If the interest is compounded often enough, will Meisha be able to buy her Porsche after only one year? Explain.

> **You make the call:** Meisha is only willing to wait 2 years to buy her new Porshe. If the best deal that Meisha can currently find is a bank which compounds interest quarterly and guarantees an annual rate of $r = 7.25\%$, what lump sum investment must Meisha make to have $80,000 in 2 years? *Hint:* Use `Goal Seek`.

1.3.3 Do We Still Need Algebra?

[Download: BreakEvenProject.xls]

It has been found through earlier research and the use of *Excel's* regression tools that FiniteFest – an annual gathering of those celebrating the beauty and utility of finite mathematics – has a price-demand function $p(t) = -0.005t + 18.5$ where $p(t)$ is the price per ticket at which t tickets can be sold. Hence $R(t) = tp(t) = t(-0.005t + 18.5)$ is the corresponding revenue function.

It has been found that organizing FiniteFest has a fixed cost of $5,000 and costs $4.50 per person in attendance. Hence, the cost of selling t tickets is given by $C(t) = 5,000 + 4.5t$. We wish to determine how many tickets need to be sold in order to break even. That is, from a mathematical point of view, we wish to find the value of t which satisfies $R(t) = C(t)$. Algebraically, we wish to solve

$$-0.005t^2 + 18.5t = 5,000 + 4.5t$$

for t. Graphically, we wish to find the two points of intersection of the revenue function $R(t)$ and the cost function $C(t)$ as shown in Figure 1.22.

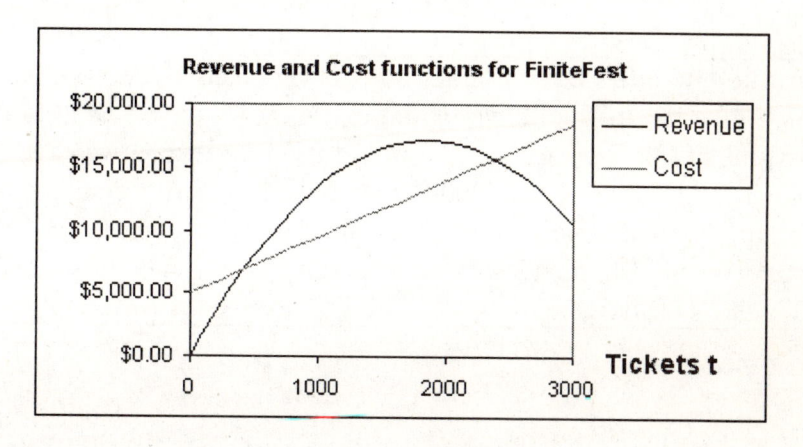

Figure 1.22: The revenue and cost functions for FiniteFest.

To solve this problem, we will attempt to use **Goal Seek**. Figure 1.23 illustrates the process. We begin with an initial value of $t = 0$ in cell **A2**. Cell **B2** representing the revenue $R(t)$ contains the formula `=-0.005*A2^2+18.5*A2`. Cell **C2** representing the cost $C(t)$ contains the formula `=5000+4.5*A2`. Since we are interested in the point where $R(t) - C(t) = 0$, we place the formula `=B2-C2` in cell **D2**. Our goal is then to set cell **D2** to a value of 0 by changing the values of t found in cell **A2**. We do this with the **Goal Seek** command under the **Tools** menu. The resulting number of tickets that will cause us to break even is approximately 420 and is shown in cell **A2**.

CHAPTER 1. FUNCTIONS, MODELS AND MORE

	A	B	C	D
1	Tickets t	Revenue R(t)	Cost C(t)	R(t)-C(t)
2	0	0	5000	-5000

Figure 1.23: Using Goal Seek to find the break even point.

1. Use Goal Seek in the spreadsheet 'Breaking Even' with an initial value of $t = 2000$ in cell A2 to approximate the number of tickets that need to be sold in order to break even.

2. The answer to the previous problem is not 420 tickets. Use Figure 1.22 to explain these two different solutions.

3. Use pencil and paper (!) and the quadratic formula to algebraically solve the equation
$$-0.005t^2 + 18.5t = 5,000 + 4.5t.$$

How many solutions did you find? Does *Excel* eliminate the need for algebra? Explain.

> **You make the call:** *Excel's* Goal Seek is very sensitive to the original input we give it. In the above example, when we gave Goal Seek an initial value of $t = 0$ we arrived at one solution and when we gave Goal Seek an initial value of $t = 2000$, we arrived at a different solution. What happens when we give Goal Seek values between 0 and 2000? In particular, what happens at an initial value of $t = 1400$? $t = 1379.9$? $t = 1379.99$? Discuss.

CHAPTER 1. FUNCTIONS, MODELS AND MORE 27

1.4 Appendix – Using the Chart Wizard

[Download: DowJonesProject.xls]

Humans are visual beasts by nature and a simple picture can greatly help in our quest to better understand data. Unlike our grandfathers and grandmothers who may have painstakingly plotted ordered pairs by hand, we have the luxury of having many different technologies at our disposal. The purpose of this appendix is to explain the simple process one uses to plot a sequence of ordered pairs in *Excel*.

Consider the data representing the Dow Jones Industrial Average (DJIA) for the years ending 1896-2000 as shown in Figure 1.24 and given in the spreadsheet 'Dow Jones Averages.'

Figure 1.24: Historical Dow Jones indices.

To plot this data, we begin by highlighting the cells A2 through B106 containing the DJIA data. Then, under the menu item Insert we find Chart. On your menu bar, you may also find the icon for the Chart Wizard as shown in Figure 1.25.

Figure 1.25: Locating the Chart Wizard in *Excel*.

Once we start the Chart Wizard, we will be asked to provide the chart type and chart sub-type. While you can experiment with the many options available to you, let's choose the XY (Scatter) plot type. Then, click Next to move on to step 2 of the plotting process. Step 2 shows you the range of the data you selected (cells A2 through B106 in this case). In step 3, we are given various options on naming the chart, identifying the axes, including a legend or not, etc... . In the final step, we

CHAPTER 1. FUNCTIONS, MODELS AND MORE 28

are asked where we would like to place the chart. When finished, a chart similar to that shown in Figure 1.26 appears. To make your chart appear as the one in Figure 1.26, simply double-click or right-click on elements of the chart you would like to change. For example, if you would like to change the background from gray to white, double-click on the gray area of the chart and change the color.

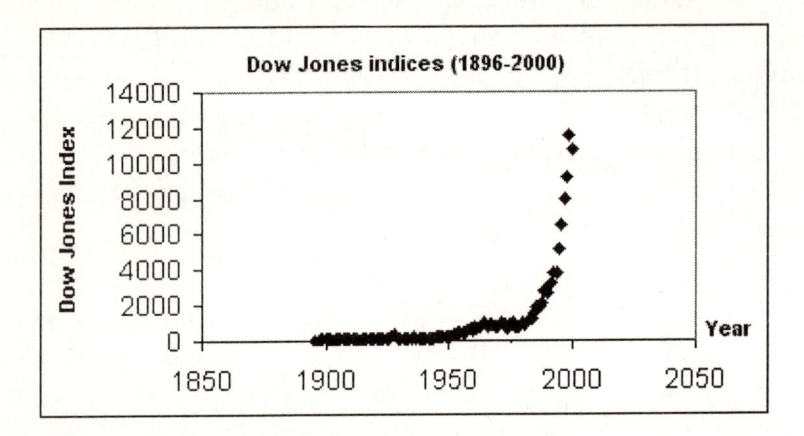

Figure 1.26: A chart representing the DJIA made by the `Chart Wizard`.

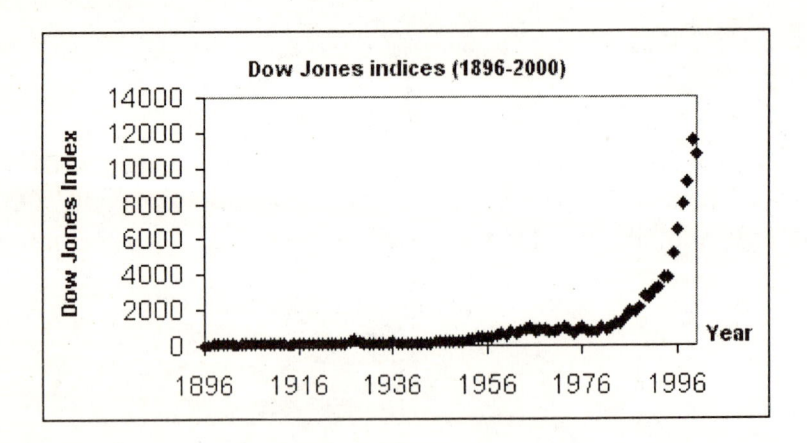

Figure 1.27: Rescaling the values on the x-axis.

One aspect of the chart that we might like to change from a mathematical point of view (rather than an asthetic one) is that of the scale of each axis. For example, we may wish to have the x-axis begin at the year 1896 and end at 2000 rather than the 1850 and 2050 values that *Excel* automatically chooses. To do this, double-click on the x-axis in the chart and choose the `Scale` tab in the `Format axis` window which appears. Change the value of `Minimum` to 1896, the value of `Maximum` to 2000, the

CHAPTER 1. FUNCTIONS, MODELS AND MORE   29

value of `Major unit` to 20, the value of `Minor unit` to 5, and uncheck all checked boxes. The new, improved(?), chart appears in Figure 1.27. Of course, the same changes may be done to the values on the y-axis.

Once you do one example using the `Chart Wizard`, play around a bit. You will find that just about anything you would like to change, you can. Basically, if you want to change it, double-click on it and you can.

Oftentimes, one would like to plot more than one set of data for comparison purposes. Suppose for example, that we would like to compare the CPI (comsumer price index) to the DJIA. Data for each of these since 1913 is given in the spreadsheet 'DJIA vs. CPI.' Since these indices had different values in 1913, we may wish to standardize the value of the CPI in another column. Since the value of the DJIA in 1913 was 78.78 and the value of the CPI that year was 9.9, we will adjust the CPI each year by multiplying it by a factor of 78.78/9.9. In *Excel*, this is done by using the formula =C2*$B$2/$C$2 in cell D2 and copying down column D. Our goal is then to plot the data in columns B and D against column A. To do this, we simply highlight these columns. The trick to doing this is the use of the `CTRL` key. Highlight the data in cells A2 through B89, hold the `CTRL` key down, and then highlight cells D2 through D89. Finally, click on the `Chart Wizard` and proceed as before. This time you will want to use a legend[9] so you can tell which index is which! Figure 1.28 gives one possible output.

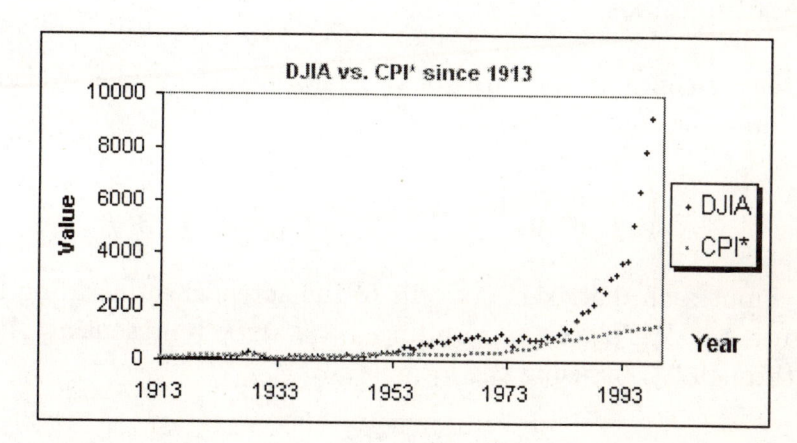

Figure 1.28: Charting the DJIA and the CPI together.

---

[9]Naming each series is done using the `Series` tab at step 2 of the plotting process.

Chapter 2

Matrices

A spreadsheet such as *Excel* is a wonderful tool for interpreting data in the form of arrays. Much of the common arithmetic that one can perform on matrices such as addition and multiplication is also easily handled by *Excel*. As this chapter will show, the power of *Excel* to perform such routine tasks frees us to search for patterns and solve more interesting mathematical problems.

2.1 Adding Matrices

[Download: AddProject.xls]

Excel can easily compute the **sum** of two matrices. Consider, for example, the problem of finding the sum $A + 2B$ where

$$A = \begin{pmatrix} 1 & 2 & 4 \\ 2 & 6 & 0 \end{pmatrix} \quad \text{and} \quad B = \begin{pmatrix} 4 & 1 & 4 \\ 0 & -1 & 3 \end{pmatrix}.$$

To begin, we input each matrix in six cells of the spreadsheet 'Adding Matrices' as shown in Figure 2.1. We place the resulting 2×3 array representing $A + 2B$ in six cells, say B6 through D7, by using the formula

$$\text{=D2+2*F2}$$

in cell B6 and copying this formula to the other cells C6, D6, B7, C7, and D7 as depicted in Figure 2.1. Note that the use of a relative reference rather than an absolute reference is critical in this process.

CHAPTER 2. MATRICES

	A	B	C	D	E	F	G	H
1		Matrix A				Matrix B		
2		1	2	4		4	1	4
3		2	6	0		0	-1	3
4								
5		Matrix A+2B						
6		9	4	12				
7		2	4	6				

Figure 2.1: Adding Matrices.

1. If
$$A = \begin{pmatrix} 1 & 2 \\ 2 & 3 \end{pmatrix} \quad \text{and} \quad B = \begin{pmatrix} 4 & 3 \\ 3 & 2 \end{pmatrix},$$
modify the spreadsheet 'Adding Matrices' shown in Figure 2.1 to compute the sum of A and B.

2. For A and B as in the previous problem, modify the spreadsheet 'Adding Matrices' to compute $-2A + 4B$.

3. The **trace** of a square matrix A is the sum of the diagonal elements. Finish designing the spreadsheet 'Trace of a Matrix' so that the trace of the 7×7 matrix appearing in cells B2 through H8 *dynamically* appears in cell B11.

> **You make the call:** In general, are the trace of a 7×7 matrix A and the trace of $\frac{1}{2}A$ related? Design a spreadsheet that will help you decide. Then, form a hypothesis about how the trace of kA is related to the trace of A for any constant k.

CHAPTER 2. MATRICES   32

2.2 Multiplying Matrices

[Download: MultiplyProject.xls]

Multiplying matrices by hand calculation is a relic of the past. *Excel* has built in machinery for computing the product of two matrices. This section describes how to use the MMULT command to solve problems that might take days without such technology.

We begin with the problem of computing the product AB of the matrices

$$A = \begin{pmatrix} 1 & 2 \\ 3 & 4 \\ 0 & 1 \end{pmatrix} \quad \text{and} \quad B = \begin{pmatrix} 4 & 3 \\ 2 & 1 \end{pmatrix}.$$

Entering **arrays**, such as a matrix, in *Excel* requires a slightly different approach than that of entering numbers. Figure 2.2 shows how we enter each matrix as an **array** in *Excel*. We begin by placing the matrix A in a block of 6 cells such as B2 through C4 as in the spreadsheet 'Matrix Multiplication.' To enter this data as an array, highlight this group of cells and simultaneously press CTRL+SHIFT+ENTER. Similarly, we enter the data for matrix B in cells E2 through F3, highlight these cells, and press CTRL+SHIFT+ENTER. To compute the 3×2 matrix product of A and B, we highlight another rectangular group of 6 cells such as B7 through C9, type

$$\text{=MMULT(B2:C4,E2:F3)}$$

and once again press CTRL+SHIFT+ENTER.

	A	B	C	D	E	F
1		Matrix A			Matrix B	
2		1	2		4	3
3		3	4		2	1
4		0	1			
5						
6		Matrix AB				
7		8	5			
8		20	13			
9		2	1			

Figure 2.2: Multiplying Matrices.

1. Modify the spreadsheet 'Matrix Multiplication' to compute the matrix product

CHAPTER 2. MATRICES

AB if

$$A = \begin{pmatrix} 1 & 2 & 4 \\ 2 & 6 & 0 \end{pmatrix} \quad \text{and} \quad B = \begin{pmatrix} 4 & 1 & 4 & 3 \\ 0 & -1 & 3 & 1 \\ 2 & 7 & 5 & 2 \end{pmatrix}.$$

2. How many cells would you need to use to place the product of a 13×7 matrix with a 7×11 matrix?

3. Let
$$A = \begin{pmatrix} 0 & 0 & 1 \\ 1 & 1 & 0 \\ 1 & 0 & 0 \end{pmatrix}.$$

   (a) Use *Excel* to compute A^2, A^4, A^8, and A^{16}.

   (b) Form a hypothesis about A^k as k grows large.

4. Let
$$B = \begin{pmatrix} 1 & 0 & 0 \\ 0 & 1 & 0 \\ a & 0 & 1 \end{pmatrix}.$$

   (a) For various values of a, use *Excel* to compute B^2, B^4, B^8, and B^{16}.

   (b) Form a hypothesis about B^k as k grows large.

5. (a) Use *Excel* to compute the matrix products AB and BA if
$$A = \begin{pmatrix} -1 & 0 \\ 2 & 3 \end{pmatrix} \quad \text{and} \quad B = \begin{pmatrix} 1 & 2 \\ 3 & 0 \end{pmatrix}.$$

   (b) Use this same spreadsheet to compute the matrix products AB and BA if
$$A = \begin{pmatrix} -1 & 0 \\ 2 & 3 \end{pmatrix} \quad \text{and} \quad B = \begin{pmatrix} 2 & 0 \\ 0 & -3 \end{pmatrix}.$$

   (c) Form a hypothesis about the products AB and BA for 2×2 matrices A and B.

6. Using the dynamic spreadsheet developed in the previous problem, compute the matrix product AB if
$$A = \begin{pmatrix} 1 & 1 \\ 1 & 1 \end{pmatrix} \quad \text{and} \quad B = \begin{pmatrix} 1 & 1 \\ -1 & -1 \end{pmatrix}.$$

Recall that for real numbers x and y, we must have either $x = 0$ or $y = 0$ if $xy = 0$. Does this same property hold for 2×2 matrices?

CHAPTER 2. MATRICES

7. (a) Use *Excel* to compute the matrix products AB and BA if

$$A = \begin{pmatrix} 2 & -1 & 3 \\ 0 & 4 & 5 \\ -2 & 1 & 4 \end{pmatrix} \quad \text{and} \quad B = \begin{pmatrix} 2 & 0 & 0 \\ 0 & 3 & 0 \\ 0 & 0 & -1 \end{pmatrix}.$$

(b) Use the same spreadsheet to compute the matrix products AB and BA if

$$A = \begin{pmatrix} 2 & -1 & 3 \\ 0 & 4 & 5 \\ -2 & 1 & 4 \end{pmatrix} \quad \text{and} \quad B = \begin{pmatrix} 4 & 0 & 0 \\ 0 & 1.5 & 0 \\ 0 & 0 & 6 \end{pmatrix}.$$

(c) Use the same spreadsheet to compute the matrix products AB and BA if

$$A = \begin{pmatrix} 2 & -1 & 3 \\ 0 & 4 & 5 \\ -2 & 1 & 4 \end{pmatrix} \quad \text{and} \quad B = \begin{pmatrix} -1 & 0 & 0 \\ 0 & 8 & 0 \\ 0 & 0 & 0 \end{pmatrix}.$$

(d) Form a hypothesis about the products AB and BA for 3×3 matrices A and B where B has the 'diagonal' form

$$B = \begin{pmatrix} a & 0 & 0 \\ 0 & b & 0 \\ 0 & 0 & c \end{pmatrix}$$

for any real numbers $a, b,$ and c.

CHAPTER 2. MATRICES

> **You make the call:** A **square root** of a matrix A is a matrix B such that $BB = A$.
>
> 1. Develop a dynamic spreadsheet that computes the product B^2 of a matrix B with itself. Use your spreadsheet to try to find a square root for the matrix
>
> $$A = \begin{pmatrix} 4 & 0 \\ 0 & 9 \end{pmatrix}.$$
>
> 2. Try to find a square root for the matrix
>
> $$A = \begin{pmatrix} 2 & 2 \\ 2 & 2 \end{pmatrix}.$$
>
> 3. Can you find more than one square root of a matrix? If so, give two square roots to the matrix
>
> $$A = \begin{pmatrix} 2 & 2 \\ 2 & 2 \end{pmatrix}.$$

2.3 Computing Inverses

[Download: InverseProject.xls]

Computing the **inverse** of a matrix by hand calculation is, as it was for matrix multiplication, a relic of the past. While it is still useful to *understand* the process of how a matrix inverse is calculated, for many applications, the numerical details involved in computing a matrix inverse are about as necessary for some students as those used in computing square roots. *Excel* has a built-in function for computing the inverse of a matrix.

Consider the (simple) problem of computing the inverse of the 3×3 matrix

$$A = \begin{pmatrix} 1 & 2 & 3 \\ 2 & 5 & 3 \\ 1 & 0 & 8 \end{pmatrix}.$$

As Figure 2.3 shows, we start by entering the matrix data in a square block of nine cells such as B2 through D4 as in the spreadsheet 'Computing an Inverse.' We enter this data as an array by highlighting this group of cells and simultaneously pressing CTRL+SHIFT+ENTER. To compute the inverse of A, we highlight another square group of nine cells such as B7 through D9, type

=MINVERSE(B2:D4)

and once again press CTRL+SHIFT+ENTER.

Notice that we now have a *dynamic* method for computing the inverse of a 3×3 matrix. That is, if we were to change the entry in the second row and third column, the (2,3) element, of the matrix from a '3' to a '4', the inverse is automatically updated!

	A	B	C	D
1		**Matrix A**		
2		1	2	3
3		2	5	3
4		1	0	8
5				
6		**Inverse of Matrix A**		
7		-40	16	9
8		13	-5	-3
9		5	-2	-1

Figure 2.3: Computing the inverse of a matrix.

CHAPTER 2. MATRICES   37

1. (a) Use the spreadsheet 'Computing an Inverse' to compute the inverse of
$$A = \begin{pmatrix} 1 & 6 & 4 \\ 2 & 4 & -1 \\ -1 & 2 & 4 \end{pmatrix}.$$

   (b) Use the same spreadsheet to compute the inverse of the slightly "perturbed" matrix
$$A = \begin{pmatrix} 1 & 6 & 4 \\ 2 & 4 & -1 \\ -1 & 2 & \boxed{5} \end{pmatrix}.$$

   (c) Form a hypothesis about how the inverse of a matrix A changes when A is "perturbed." To help in forming a hypothesis, try changing the (3,3) entry of A to 4.99, 4.999, and 4.9999 successively.

2. (a) Use the spreadsheet 'Computing an Inverse' to compute the inverse of
$$A = \begin{pmatrix} 1 & 0 & 0 \\ 0 & 1 & 0 \\ -0.6 & 9 & 1 \end{pmatrix}.$$

   (b) Use the same spreadsheet to compute the inverse of the matrix
$$A = \begin{pmatrix} 1 & 0 & 0 \\ 0 & 1 & 0 \\ 4 & -5 & 1 \end{pmatrix}.$$

   (c) By experimenting with various values of a and b, form a hypothesis about the inverse of a matrix A having the form
$$A = \begin{pmatrix} 1 & 0 & 0 \\ 0 & 1 & 0 \\ a & b & 1 \end{pmatrix}.$$
   where a and b are any real numbers.

3. (a) Use the spreadsheet 'Computing an Inverse' to compute the inverse of
$$A = \begin{pmatrix} 2 & 0 & 0 \\ 0 & -4 & 0 \\ 0 & 0 & 0.5 \end{pmatrix}.$$

CHAPTER 2. MATRICES

(b) Use the same spreadsheet to compute the inverse of the matrix

$$A = \begin{pmatrix} 1 & 0 & 0 \\ 0 & 4 & 0 \\ 0 & 0 & -1.4 \end{pmatrix}.$$

(c) By experimenting with various values of a, b, and c, form a hypothesis about the inverse of a matrix A having the 'diagonal' form

$$A = \begin{pmatrix} a & 0 & 0 \\ 0 & b & 0 \\ 0 & 0 & c \end{pmatrix}.$$

where a,b, and c are any real numbers.

4. (a) Use the spreadsheet 'Computing an Inverse' to compute the inverse of

$$A = \begin{pmatrix} 1 & 2 & 3 \\ 0 & 1 & 2 \\ 0 & 0 & 1 \end{pmatrix}.$$

(b) Modify the spreadsheet to compute the inverse of the matrix

$$A = \begin{pmatrix} 1 & 2 & 3 & 4 \\ 0 & 1 & 2 & 3 \\ 0 & 0 & 1 & 2 \\ 0 & 0 & 0 & 1 \end{pmatrix}.$$

(c) Further modify this spreadsheet to compute the inverse of the matrix

$$A = \begin{pmatrix} 1 & 2 & 3 & 4 & 5 \\ 0 & 1 & 2 & 3 & 4 \\ 0 & 0 & 1 & 2 & 3 \\ 0 & 0 & 0 & 1 & 2 \\ 0 & 0 & 0 & 0 & 1 \end{pmatrix}.$$

(d) Form a hypothesis based on your findings. Does your hypothesis hold on the next 6×6 matrix in this sequence?

5. (a) As we have seen, when multiplying matrices order is very important. If a square matrix A is invertible, can we take the inverse of A and the square of A in either order? That is, is it always true that $(A^2)^{-1} = (A^{-1})^2$? To test this hypothesis, try various 3×3 matrices A in the spreadsheet 'Powers of Inverses.'

CHAPTER 2. MATRICES

(b) Test the hypothesis that $(A^2)^{-1} = (A^{-1})^2$ for various 4×4 matrices A. You will need to design a spreadsheet similar to 'Powers of Inverses.'

6. (a) If square matrices A and B are invertible, is it always true that $(AB)^{-1} = A^{-1}B^{-1}$? To test this hypothesis, try various 3×3 matrices A and B in the spreadsheet 'Products of Inverses.'

   (b) Test the hypothesis that $(AB)^{-1} = A^{-1}B^{-1}$ for various 4×4 matrices A and B. You will need to design a spreadsheet similar to 'Products of Inverses.'

CHAPTER 2. MATRICES

You make the call: An $n \times n$ **circulant matrix** A is defined to be a matrix in which for some $1 \leq i \leq n$, $A_{i,(i+k) \bmod n}$ is a constant a for $1 \leq k \leq n-1$ and all other entries of A are zero. An example (in simple terms!) would be the 4×4 matrix

$$A = \begin{pmatrix} 0 & 2 & 0 & 0 \\ 0 & 0 & 2 & 0 \\ 0 & 0 & 0 & 2 \\ 2 & 0 & 0 & 0 \end{pmatrix}.$$

Notice how the 2's form a superdiagonal that 'wraps around' when it reaches the right side of the array.

1. Using the spreadsheet 'Circulant Matrices,' compute the inverse of the 5×5 circulant matrix

$$A = \begin{pmatrix} 0 & 4 & 0 & 0 & 0 \\ 0 & 0 & 4 & 0 & 0 \\ 0 & 0 & 0 & 4 & 0 \\ 0 & 0 & 0 & 0 & 4 \\ 4 & 0 & 0 & 0 & 0 \end{pmatrix}.$$

2. Using the same spreadsheet, compute the inverse of the 5×5 circulant matrix

$$A = \begin{pmatrix} 0 & 0 & 5 & 0 & 0 \\ 0 & 0 & 0 & 5 & 0 \\ 0 & 0 & 0 & 0 & 5 \\ 5 & 0 & 0 & 0 & 0 \\ 0 & 5 & 0 & 0 & 0 \end{pmatrix}.$$

3. Form a hypothesis about the inverse of an $n \times n$ circulant matrix A based on your findings. Verify your hypothesis on a 6×6 circulant matrix of your choice.

2.4 Solving Linear Systems

[Download: LinearSystemProject.xls]

Excel is an excellent tool for solving matrix equations of the form $Ax = b$ where A is a square matrix and has an inverse. You may recall that the (unique) solution is given by the matrix product $x = A^{-1}b$. Hence, by putting together the MINVERSE and MMULT commands, we can solve such systems. We illustrate this process with an example.

Consider the problem of solving the matrix equation

$$\begin{pmatrix} 1 & 2 & 3 \\ 2 & 5 & 3 \\ 1 & 0 & 8 \end{pmatrix} \begin{pmatrix} x \\ y \\ z \end{pmatrix} = \begin{pmatrix} 4 \\ 5 \\ 9 \end{pmatrix}.$$

Of course, we can think of this equation as $Ax = b$ where

$$A = \begin{pmatrix} 1 & 2 & 3 \\ 2 & 5 & 3 \\ 1 & 0 & 8 \end{pmatrix}, \quad x = \begin{pmatrix} x \\ y \\ z \end{pmatrix}, \text{ and } b = \begin{pmatrix} 4 \\ 5 \\ 9 \end{pmatrix}.$$

The spreadsheet 'Solving $Ax = b$' shown in Figure 2.4 exhibits a possible solution process. The idea is quite simple. Since we know the solution will be a 3×1 matrix, we simply highlight cells B7 through B9, type

=MMULT(MINVERSE(B2:D4),F2:F4),

and enter the array by pressing CTRL+SHIFT+ENTER as usual.

	A	B	C	D	E	F
1		Matrix A				b
2		1	2	3		4
3		2	5	3		5
4		1	0	8		9
5						
6		Solution x				
7		1				
8		0				
9		1				

Figure 2.4: Solving $Ax = b$ when A is invertible.

Notice how *dynamic* this process is. If we change the elements in the matrix b to $(1,6,-6)$, the solution x instantly updates itself to $(2,1,-1)$. This is very useful as the solution x can often be sensitive to changes in input A and b.

CHAPTER 2. MATRICES

2.4.1 Computing Return on Investment by Catagory

[Download: CatagoryReturnProject.xls]

As an investor, you have invested in five mutual funds. These funds are each invested in five different types of vehicles: international stock, domestic stock, corporate bonds, government bonds, and cash equivalents. The matrix in the spreadsheet 'Catagory Return' shown in Figure 2.5 describes how much each fund invests in each catagory. By solving a matrix system $Ax = b$ (via the spreadsheet) we can determine the return from each of the 5 types of investment vehicles.

	International Stock	Domestic Stock	Corporate Bonds	Government Bonds	Cash Equivalent
Fund A	10.0%	20.0%	5.0%	50.0%	15.0%
Fund B	60.0%	40.0%	0.0%	0.0%	0.0%
Fund C	20.0%	20.0%	20.0%	20.0%	20.0%
Fund D	40.0%	20.0%	10.0%	25.0%	5.0%
Fund E	5.0%	5.0%	30.0%	40.0%	20.0%

Figure 2.5: Return on investment by catagory for five mutual funds.

If the percentage return in Fund A was 6%, the return in Fund B was 10%, the return in Fund C was 8%, the return in Fund D was 7%, and the return in Fund E was 5%, determine the return on domestic stock by using the spreadsheet 'Catagory Return' to solve a matrix equation $Ax = b$.

> **You make the call:** If the return of Fund E was misreported and was actually 6% rather than 5%, what was the actual return on domestic stock? Is this a good method for investors to use in calculating return by investment vehicle? Discuss.

2.4.2 Planning a Daily Diet

[Download: DailyDietProject.xls]

A dietician wishes to plan a daily diet around eight foods. Each ounce of food 1 contains 10% of the daily requirements for nutrient 1, 10% of the daily requirements for nutrient 2, 15% of the daily requirements for nutrient 3, 4% of the daily requirements for nutrient 4, 0% of the daily requirements for nutrient 5, 16% of the daily requirements for nutrient 6, 3% of the daily requirements for nutrient 7, and 0% of the daily requirements for nutrient 8. These percentages are given in row 1 of the matrix in the spreadsheet of Figure 2.6. Percentages of the daily requirements for foods 2 through 8 are given in rows 2 through 8 of the same matrix in the spreadsheet 'Daily Diet' shown in Figure 2.6.

Use this spreadsheet to compute how many ounces of each food should be served in order to exactly supply the daily requirements for the eight nutrients.

		Nutrient #								Daily Requirement
		1	2	3	4	5	6	7	8	
Food #	1	10%	10%	15%	4%	0%	16%	3%	0%	100%
	2	20%	12%	0%	5%	2%	20%	25%	0%	100%
	3	2%	1%	20%	1%	0%	0%	40%	15%	100%
	4	0%	6%	10%	0%	10%	30%	30%	0%	100%
	5	0%	11%	0%	20%	40%	15%	10%	0%	100%
	6	14%	10%	12%	0%	20%	3%	0%	10%	100%
	7	8%	0%	0%	14%	0%	6%	2%	35%	100%
	8	5%	0%	5%	3%	0%	50%	2%	0%	100%

Figure 2.6: Planning a daily diet.

> **You make the call:** Use the data in the spreadsheet 'Daily Diet' to determine how many ounces of each food should be served if the diet requires exactly 200% of the daily requirement for nutrient 5.

CHAPTER 2. MATRICES

2.4.3 The Hilbert Matrix

[Download: HilbertProject.xls]

Solutions x to the matrix equation $Ax = b$ can be sensitive both to changes in the entries of the matrix A and to changes in b. One particular matrix that illustrates this well is called the **Hilbert matrix**. The $(i,j)^{th}$ entry of an $n \times n$ Hilbert matrix H is defined by $H_{i,j} = \frac{1}{i+j-1}$. A 5×5 Hilbert matrix as shown in Figure 2.7 has been entered in the spreadsheet 'Hilbert Matrix.'

1	1/2	1/3	1/4	1/5
1/2	1/3	1/4	1/5	1/6
1/3	1/4	1/5	1/6	1/7
1/4	1/5	1/6	1/7	1/8
1/5	1/6	1/7	1/8	1/9

Figure 2.7: A 5×5 Hilbert matrix.

1. Using the spreadsheet 'Hilbert Matrix,' compare the solution of the matrix equation $Hx = (1, 1, 1, 1, 1)$ with that of $Hx = (1, 1, 1, 1, 0.9)$. How do these solutions compare to the solution of $Hx = (1, 1, 1, 1, 0.99)$? $Hx = (1, 1, 1, 1, 0.999)$?

2. Suppose now we change an entry of the matrix H. Call H' the matrix H with the (5,5) element changed to $1/10$ from $1/9$. How does the solution of $H'x = (1, 1, 1, 1, 1)$ compare with that of $H'x = (1, 1, 1, 1, 1)$?

> **You make the call:** Suppose that $b = (1, 1, 1, 1, 1)$ represented a set of measurements and that each had error as little as 0.0001. How far off might the solution to $Hx = b$ be from the true solution?

CHAPTER 2. MATRICES

2.5 Gauss-Jordan Elimination

[Download: RREFProject.xls]

It is often the case that in looking for solutions to the matrix equation $Ax = b$, A is not invertible (or even square!). In these cases, we commonly use **Gauss-Jordan elimination** to put the augmented matrix $(A|b)$ in **reduced row echelon form**. The spreadsheet 'Row Operations' illustrates how row operations can be applied to "small" matrices A. For larger matrices A, using other computer software is a much better approach.

Consider the augmented matrix

$$\begin{pmatrix} 2 & -4 & 1 & | & -4 \\ 4 & -8 & 7 & | & 2 \\ -2 & 4 & -3 & | & 5 \end{pmatrix}.$$

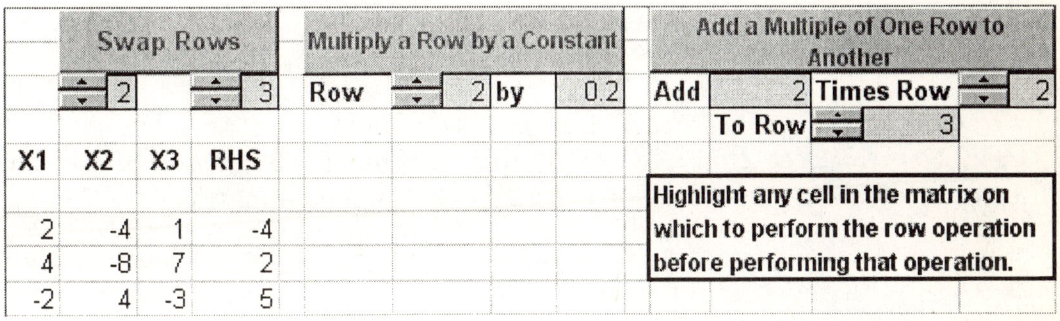

Figure 2.8: Performing row operations on a matrix using the spreadsheet 'Row Operations.'

Using the spreadsheet 'Row Operations' as shown in Figure 2.8, we can reduce this matrix using Gauss-Jordan elimination to reduced row echelon form using the following operations in the given order:

$$\begin{aligned} 0.5R_1 &\to R_1 \\ -4R_1 + R_2 &\to R_2 \\ 2R_1 + R_3 &\to R_3 \\ 0.2R_2 &\to R_2 \\ -0.5R_2 + R_1 &\to R_1 \\ 2R_2 + R_3 &\to R_3 \end{aligned}$$

CHAPTER 2. MATRICES

After these operations are performed, we arrive at the equivalent augmented matrix

$$\begin{pmatrix} 1 & -2 & 0 & | & -3 \\ 0 & 0 & 1 & | & 2 \\ 0 & 0 & 0 & | & 5 \end{pmatrix}.$$

From this, it is clear that the original system of equations has no solution since the last row is inconsistent.

1. Use the spreadsheet 'Row Operations' to reduce the augmented matrix

$$\begin{pmatrix} 2 & -4 & 1 & | & -4 \\ 4 & -8 & 7 & | & 2 \\ -2 & 4 & -3 & | & \boxed{0} \end{pmatrix}$$

to row reduced echelon form. Compare *how many* solutions this system has to the number of solutions of a very 'similar' system described by the augmented matrix

$$\begin{pmatrix} 2 & -4 & 1 & | & -4 \\ 4 & -8 & 7 & | & 2 \\ -2 & 4 & -3 & | & \boxed{0.1} \end{pmatrix}.$$

2. Use the spreadsheet 'Row Operations' to help compare the *number* of solutions for the systems of equations described by the augmented matrices

$$\begin{pmatrix} 1 & 2 & -3 & | & 5 \\ 2 & 4 & \boxed{-6} & | & 10 \\ -2 & -3 & 4 & | & -6 \end{pmatrix}$$

and

$$\begin{pmatrix} 1 & 2 & -3 & | & 5 \\ 2 & 4 & \boxed{-6.01} & | & 10 \\ -2 & -3 & 4 & | & -6 \end{pmatrix}.$$

> **You make the call:** What happens to a unique solution of the system $Ax = b$ when a row operation is performed on the augmented matrix $(A|b)$? Using the spreadsheet 'Solutions After Row Operations,' form a hypothesis as to what happens to solutions x when various row operations are applied to the matrix $(A|b)$.

2.6 The Transpose

[Download: TransposeProject.xls]

Much like computing matrix inverses, *Excel* has a built-in function for computing the **transpose** of a matrix.

We begin with the problem of computing the transpose of the 3×4 matrix

$$A = \begin{pmatrix} 1 & 2 & 3 & 4 \\ 2 & 5 & 3 & -1 \\ 1 & 0 & 8 & 9 \end{pmatrix}.$$

We enter the matrix A as a 3×4 block of 12 cells (say in cells `B2` through `E4`) as we did when we used *Excel* to compute matrix inverses and matrix products by highlighting the array and simultaneously pressing `CTRL+SHIFT+ENTER`. To compute the transpose of A, we highlight a 4×3 block of 12 cells, type

```
=TRANSPOSE(B2:E4)
```

and once again press `CTRL+SHIFT+ENTER`. The spreadsheet 'Transposing a Matrix' shown in Figure 2.9 exhibits this process.

	A	B	C	D	E	F	G	H	I
1		Matrix A					Transpose of A		
2		1	2	3	4		1	2	1
3		2	5	3	-1		2	5	0
4		1	0	8	9		3	3	8
5							4	-1	9

Figure 2.9: Computing the transpose of a matrix.

1. If a square matrix A is invertible, can we take the inverse of A and the transpose of A in either order? Put another way, is it true that $(A^T)^{-1} = (A^{-1})^T$?
   (a) To test this hypothesis, try various 3×3 matrices A in the spreadsheet 'Transposes and Inverses.'
   (b) Test the hypothesis that $(A^T)^{-1} = (A^{-1})^T$ for various 4×4 matrices A. You will need to design a spreadsheet similar to 'Transposes and Inverses.'

CHAPTER 2. MATRICES

2. If A is an $m \times n$ matrix and b is $m \times 1$, we cannot always find a unique solution to the matrix equation $Ax = b$ (i.e. $Ax - b = 0$). Suppose however, that we want the "best" solution (called the **least squares solution**) in the following sense. We want to find x so that $y = Ax - b$ is as 'small as possible.' Technically, we want to find an $x = (x_1, x_2, ..., x_n)$ such that

$$\sqrt{y_1^2 + y_2^2 + ... + y_n^2}$$

is as small as possible. It turns out that such an x can be found by solving the matrix equation $A^T Ax = A^T b$.

(a) Use the spreadsheet 'Least Squares' to compute the least squares solution to $Ax = b$ where

$$A = \begin{pmatrix} 1 & 1 \\ 1 & -1 \\ 1 & 2 \end{pmatrix} \quad \text{and} \quad b = \begin{pmatrix} 2 \\ 0 \\ 5 \end{pmatrix}.$$

What happens when you try to find the actual solution to $Ax = b$ by hand?

(b) Use the spreadsheet 'Least Squares' to compute the least squares solution to $Ax = b$ where

$$A = \begin{pmatrix} 1 & 1 \\ 1 & -1 \\ 2 & 2 \end{pmatrix} \quad \text{and} \quad b = \begin{pmatrix} 2 \\ 0 \\ 4 \end{pmatrix}.$$

What happens when you try to find the actual solution to $Ax = b$ by hand?

(c) Use the spreadsheet 'Least Squares' to determine what happens when you try to find the least squares solution to $Ax = b$ where

$$A = \begin{pmatrix} 1 & 1 \\ 2 & 2 \\ 3 & 3 \end{pmatrix} \quad \text{and} \quad b = \begin{pmatrix} 2 \\ 4 \\ 6 \end{pmatrix}.$$

Why is this case so different from the two cases above? Does $Ax = b$ have a least squares solution? Does it have a solution?

You make the call: For *any* rectangular matrix A, is there anything that can be said about the structure of that matrix product $A^T A$? Experiment with various 2×3 matrices A in the spreadsheet 'Transpose Times A' in order to form a hypothesis regarding the structure of the matrix product $A^T A$. Try modifying this spreadsheet in such a way to verify your hypothesis for several 2×4 matrices A.

CHAPTER 2. MATRICES 49

2.7 Determinants

[Download: DeterminantProject.xls]

Excel has a built-in function for computing the **determinant** of a matrix. This function is very easy to use. Simply enter a matrix in an array of cells, say B2 through E5, and in a single new cell enter the formula

$$\text{=MDETERM(B2:D4)}$$

as in the spreadsheet 'Computing Determinants' shown in Figure 2.10.

	A	B	C	D	E	F	G
1		Matrix A					Determinant
2		3	1	4	2		368
3		-1	2	0	5		
4		4	3	0	-1		
5		0	4	2	1		

Figure 2.10: Computing the determinant of a 4×4 matrix.

1. The spreadsheet 'Determinants and Transposes' computes the determinant of a 4×4 matrix A and its transpose A^T.

    (a) By changing various entries of the matrix A, form a hypothesis about how $det(A)$ and $det(A^T)$ are related.

    (b) Test the hypothesis that you made above for various 5×5 matrices A. You will need to design a spreadsheet similar to 'Determinants and Transposes.'

2. For a square matrix A, if $det(A) \neq 0$, then A has an inverse. Is there a relationship between $det(A)$ and $det(A^{-1})$?

    (a) Use the spreadsheet 'Determinants and Inverses' which simultaneously computes the determinant of 3×3 matrices A and A^{-1} to compute $det(A)$ and $det(A^{-1})$ if

    $$A = \begin{pmatrix} 3 & 1 & 2 \\ 1 & 2 & 3 \\ 1 & 1 & 1 \end{pmatrix}.$$

    (b) Using the spreadsheet 'Determinants and Inverses,' gather data in order to form a hypothesis about how $det(A)$ and $det(A^{-1})$ are related. Can you see why it is important that $det(A) \neq 0$?

CHAPTER 2. MATRICES 50

3. Is it true that for square matrices A and B of the same size, that we always have $det(AB) = det(A)det(B)$? Is it always the case that $det(A + B) = det(A) + det(B)$? Using various inputs for 3×3 matrices A and B, experiment with the spreadsheets 'Determinants and Products' and 'Determinants and Sums' to speculate about these two hypotheses.

> **You make the call:** For a 3×3 matrix A and a real number k, is there a relationship between $det(kA)$ and $det(A)$? Experiment with various matrices A in the spreadsheet 'Determinants and Multiples' which simultaneously computes the $det(kA)$ and $det(A)$ to form a hypothesis about how $det(kA)$ and $det(A)$ are related.

2.8 Leontief Input-Output Analysis

[Download: InputOutputProject.xls]

Imagine an economy based on four sectors, agriculture (A), energy (E), labor (L), and manufacturing (M). The data entered in the spreadsheet 'Input-Output Analysis' shown in Figure 2.11 gives the input requirements for a dollar's worth of output for each sector, along with the projected final demand (in billions of dollars) for a particular year. The basic problem we are confronted with is to find the output for each sector that is needed to satisfy each of these final demands.

	A	B	C	D	E	F	G	H	I	J	K	L	M
1			Output					Final Demand		Identity Matrix			
2			A	E	L	M							
3	Input	A	0.05	0.17	0.23	0.09		$23.00		1	0	0	0
4		E	0.07	0.12	0.15	0.19		$41.00		0	1	0	0
5		L	0.25	0.08	0.03	0.32		$18.00		0	0	1	0
6		M	0.11	0.19	0.28	0.16		$31.00		0	0	0	1
7													
8										I-M (Identity - Technology Matrix)			
9										0.95	-0.17	-0.23	-0.09
10										-0.07	0.88	-0.15	-0.19
11										-0.25	-0.08	0.97	-0.32
12										-0.11	-0.19	-0.28	0.84
13													
14										Output Matrix			
15									A	$64.51			
16									E	$82.75			
17									L	$70.94			
18									M	$87.72			

Figure 2.11: A Leontief Input-Output Analysis.

To construct this *Excel* worksheet, we entered the **technology matrix** M in cells C3 through F6 and we entered the **final demand matrix** D in cells H3 through H6. Then, in order to compute the **output matrix**, we enter the 4×4 identity matrix in cells J3 through M6. We let the spreadsheet compute $I - M$ (the identity - the technology matrix) in cells J9 through M12 placing the command =J3-C3 in cell J9 and copying this formula to the required cells. Finally, we compute the output matrix in cells J15 through J18 by highlighting these cells, typing

=MMULT(MINVERSE(J9:M12),H3:H6),

CHAPTER 2. MATRICES

and pressing CTRL+SHIFT+ENTER.

The following problems involve the economy given in the spreadsheet 'Input-Output Analysis.'

1. For this economy, what effect does a doubling of the final demand for energy (E) have on the manufacturing output needed to reach this new demand?

2. Suppose that the amount of energy (E) needed to produce one unit of agriculture (A) is cut in half. What effect does this have on the manufacturing output level?

3. Suppose all the industries (A), (E), (L), and (M) cut the amount of energy (E) needed to produce one unit of output in half. What effect does this have on the manufacturing output?

4. If all four industries cut the amount of energy (E) needed to produce one unit of output in half *and* the final demand for energy (E) increases to $60 billion, which industries need to increase output levels to reach this new demand? if the demand for energy (E) increases to $61 billion?

> **You make the call:** Use the spreadsheet 'Input-Output Analysis' to determine what happens in the strange scenario that the final demand for this economy is $1 billion of agriculture (A) and no final demand for energy (E), labor (L), and manufacturing (M).

Chapter 3

Linear Programming

In this chapter, we will use *Excel's* built-in `Solver` to solve some linear (and integer and nonlinear!) programming problems. In order to do this, the `Solver` add-in must be installed. Typically, this feature is not installed by default when *Excel* is first setup on a computer. To add this facility to the `Tools` menu, consult the appendix at the end of this chapter.

3.1 The McDonald's Diet

[Download: McDonaldsProject.xls]

Ronald only eats at McDonald's restaurants. Depending on his mood, he either wants to minimize his cost, minimize his fat intake, or maximize his calorie intake. There are six staple foods in Ronald's diet: hamburgers, french fries, garden salads, crispy chicken sandwiches, milk, and Diet Coke. Data regarding these McDonald's foods is shown in Figure 3.1.[1] The question we would like to answer is "Given a particular mood that Ronald is in, how can we satisfy Ronald's desires?".

Food	Cost	Fat (g)	Protein (g)	Calories
Hamburger	$0.89	10	12	280
Medium French Fries	$1.19	22	6	210
Garden Salad	$2.49	10	7	100
Crispy Chicken	$1.39	27	23	550
1% Milk (carton)	$0.69	2.5	8	100
Medium Diet Coke	$0.99	0	0	0

Figure 3.1: Data for Ronald's diet.

---

[1]Data from www.mcdonalds.com

CHAPTER 3. LINEAR PROGRAMMING 54

In the spreadsheet 'Minimizing Cost,' the formula

$$=C3*H3+C4*H4+C5*H5+C6*H6+C7*H7+C8*H8$$

has been placed in cell C10. This formula computes the price of a meal as a function of how many of each item is purchased. Similar formulas appear in cells E14 through E16.

	A	B	C	D	E	F	G	H
2	Food		Cost	Fat (g)	Protein (g)	Calories		Number
3	Hamburger		$0.89	10	12	280		1
4	Medium French Fries		$1.19	22	6	210		1
5	Garden Salad		$2.49	10	7	100		1
6	Crispy Chicken		$1.39	27	23	550		1
7	1% Milk (carton)		$0.69	2.5	8	100		1
8	Medium Diet Coke		$0.99	0	0	0		1
9								
10	Minimize Cost		$7.64					
11								
12	Subject to				Values at Optimal Solution			
13								
14	Calorie Requirement (>=)		2000		1240			
15	Fat Requirement (<=)		80		71.5			
16	Protein Requirement (>=)		20		56			

Figure 3.2: Ronald's set up for the Solver.

As an example, our first goal for Ronald will be to minimize his cost subject to the conditions that he eat at least 2000 calories, eat less than 80 grams of fat, and eat at least 20 grams of protein. The variables in this problem are the number of menu items of each type he orders. That is,

x_1 = number of hamburgers Ronald orders
x_2 = number of medium french fries Ronald orders
x_3 = number of garden salads Ronald orders
x_4 = number of crispy chickens Ronald orders
x_5 = number of cartons of milk Ronald orders
x_6 = number of medium Diet Cokes Ronald orders

CHAPTER 3. LINEAR PROGRAMMING

We can mathematically state our problem as

$$\text{Minimize} \quad C = 0.89x_1 + 1.19x_2 + 2.49x_3 + 1.39x_4 + 0.69x_5 + 0.99x_6$$
$$\text{subject to} \quad 280x_1 + 210x_2 + 100x_3 + 550x_4 + 100x_5 + 0x_6 \geq 2000$$
$$10x_1 + 22x_2 + 10x_3 + 27x_4 + 2.5x_5 + 0x_6 \leq 80$$
$$12x_1 + 6x_2 + 7x_3 + 23x_4 + 8x_5 + 0x_6 \geq 20$$
$$x_i \geq 0 \ (i = 1, 2, ..., 6)$$
$$x_i \text{ integer}$$

We begin by inputing the parameters 2000, 80, and 20 in cells C14, C15, and C16. Then, in order to solve a particular optimization problem, we select Solver under the the menu option Tools. When the Solver Parameters window pops up (see Figure 3.3), we select the desired input.

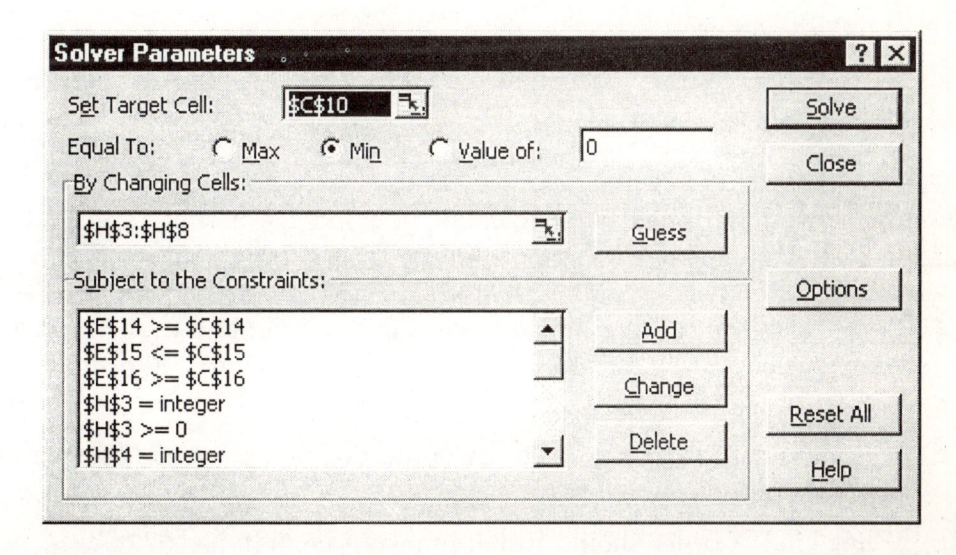

Figure 3.3: Entering the objective function and constraints into the Solver Parameters window.

In the Solver window, we set the target cell as C10 since this is what we are trying to minimize. We will minimize our cost by changing cells H3:H8 containing the values for the variables $x_1, x_2, ..., x_6$. Next, we input our requirements for a feasible solution. For example, the condition that we have at least 2000 calories in Ronald's diet translates to the constraint E14 >= C14. As another example, the condition that we order a nonnegative integer number of medium Diet Cokes translates to the constraints H8 >= 0 and H8 = Integer. The other required conditions for this problems are input into the spreadsheet for you. Finally, we hit Solve and let *Excel*

CHAPTER 3. LINEAR PROGRAMMING

do its job. *Excel* tells us that Ronald should order 5 hamburgers, 1 crispy chicken sandwich, and 1 carton of milk!

1. Before solving any of Ronald's problems, decide whether or not Ronald will ever be in a mood to order Diet Coke. Explain.

2. Suppose that Ronald is in a mood to minimize his costs. Use the spreadsheet 'Minimizing Cost' and *Excel's* Solver to answer the following.

    (a) If we require that Ronald eat at least 2000 calories, eat less than 80 grams of fat, and eat at least 20 grams of protein, what is the minimum this will cost Ronald? How much protein does Ronald actually get by making these choices in ordering?

    (b) If Ronald is a growing boy and needs at least 2800 calories (while still eating less than 80 grams of fat and at least 20 grams of protein), what should he order?

    (c) If Ronald goes on a 'diet' and only needs 1000 calories a day and is restricted to less than 25 grams of fat per day, what should he order to minimize his costs? How much does this cost? Is this a good 'diet'?

3. Suppose now that Ronald is in a mood to minimize his fat intake. Use the spreadsheet 'Minimizing Fat Intake' and *Excel's* Solver to answer the following.

    (a) If we require that Ronald eat at least 2000 calories and that he eat at least 20 grams of protein for under $10.00, what should Ronald order? What is his fat intake with this order?

    (b) If Ronald has only half of the $10.00 needed above, what happens? Interpret this output.

    (c) What kind of order should Ronald make if he only has $7.00?

    (d) With $10.00, would Ronald ever order a garden salad to minimize his fat intake? Explain.

4. Suppose that Ronald is in a mood to maximize his caloric intake. Use the spreadsheet 'Maximizing Calorie Intake' and *Excel's* Solver to answer the following.

    (a) If we require that Ronald eat at most 40 grams of fat and that he eat at least 20 grams of protein for under $5.00, what should Ronald order?

    (b) Suppose Ronald does not care if he keeps his diet to under 40 grams of fat, but rather he wished to keep it under 100 grams of fat. What should Ronald order now? Does this make sense? Why?

CHAPTER 3. LINEAR PROGRAMMING

(c) If there were a $0.39 sale on medium french fries and Ronald (with $5.00) does not care how much fat he eats, what should he order? To make sense out of this answer, in column J, calculate the calories per unit cost of each food item. What do you notice?

> **You make the call:** Suppose that Ronald insists on ordering at least one Diet Coke and that he wishes to otherwise minimize the cost of his order. If we require that Ronald eat at least 2000 calories, eat less than 80 grams of fat, and eat at least 20 grams of protein, what else should Ronald order? How much would his order cost?

CHAPTER 3. LINEAR PROGRAMMING   58

3.2 Petroleum Blending

[Download: PetroleumBlendingProject.xls]

The Gas-Iz-Us refinery produces three grades of gasoline (regular unleaded, super unleaded, and premium unleaded) by blending together three components: A, B, and C. The components, their octane ratings, their price per barrel, and the supply of each available are shown in Figure 3.4.

Component	Octane	Cost ($)	Available Supply (barrels)
A	90	$30.00	30,000
B	105	$32.50	10,000
C	110	$34.00	25,000

Figure 3.4: Requirements on petroleum input.

Information regarding the demand of the gasoline products to be produced is shown in Figure 3.5.

Grade	Minimum Octane	Selling Price ($)	Demand (barrels)
Regular	95	$36.00	20,000
Super	97	$37.00	20,000
Premium	105	$44.00	5,000

Figure 3.5: Information regarding petroleum output.

The obvious question that the refinery has is "How should we blend these components so as to satisfy demand and maximize profits?". We begin by identifying the variables to be used in solving this problem. We have

x_1 = number of barrels of component A used in regular
x_2 = number of barrels of component A used in super
x_3 = number of barrels of component A used in premium
x_4 = number of barrels of component B used in regular
x_5 = number of barrels of component B used in super
x_6 = number of barrels of component B used in premium
x_7 = number of barrels of component C used in regular
x_8 = number of barrels of component C used in super
x_9 = number of barrels of component C used in premium

CHAPTER 3. LINEAR PROGRAMMING

	A	B	C	D	E
2	Component		Octane	Cost ($)	Available Supply (barrels)
3	A		90	$30.00	30,000
4	B		105	$32.50	10,000
5	C		110	$34.00	25,000
6					
7	Grade		Minimum Octane	Selling Price ($)	Demand (barrels)
8	Regular		95	$36.00	20,000
9	Super		97	$37.00	20,000
10	Premium		105	$44.00	5,000
11					
12	Variables				Optimum Mix
13	Number of barrels of A used in Regular				30000
14	Number of barrels of A used in Super				0
15	Number of barrels of A used in Premium				0
16	Number of barrels of B used in Regular				0
17	Number of barrels of B used in Super				10000
18	Number of barrels of B used in Premium				0
19	Number of barrels of C used in Regular				0
20	Number of barrels of C used in Super				0
21	Number of barrels of C used in Premium				25000
22					
23	Maximize		$475,000.00		
24					
25	Subject to				
26					Values
27	Supply of A (<=)			30,000	30000.0
28	Supply of B (<=)			10,000	10000.0
29	Supply of C (<=)			25,000	25000.0
30	Demand for A (>=)			20,000	30000.0
31	Demand for B (>=)			20,000	10000.0
32	Demand for C (>=)			5,000	25000.0
33	Octane Rating for Regular (>=)			95	90
34	Octane Rating for Super (>=)			97	105
35	Octane Rating for Premium (>=)			105	110

Figure 3.6: Setting up to use the `Solver` on the petroleum blending problem.

Realizing that profit is revenue less costs, we then mathematically state our problem as

Maximize

$$P = 36(x_1 + x_4 + x_7) + 37(x_2 + x_5 + x_8) + 44(x_3 + x_6 + x_9) \\ - 30(x_1 + x_2 + x_3) - 32.5(x_4 + x_5 + x_6) - 34(x_7 + x_8 + x_9)$$

subject to

$$\left\{ \begin{array}{rcl} x_1 + x_2 + x_3 & \leq & 30,000 \\ x_4 + x_5 + x_6 & \leq & 10,000 \\ x_7 + x_8 + x_9 & \leq & 25,000 \end{array} \right\} \text{ supply constraints}$$

$$\left\{ \begin{array}{rcl} x_1 + x_4 + x_7 & \geq & 20,000 \\ x_2 + x_5 + x_8 & \geq & 20,000 \\ x_3 + x_6 + x_9 & \geq & 5,000 \end{array} \right\} \text{ demand constraints}$$

$$\left\{ \begin{array}{rcl} 90\frac{x_1}{x_1+x_4+x_7} + 105\frac{x_4}{x_1+x_4+x_7} + 110\frac{x_7}{x_1+x_4+x_7} & \geq & 95 \\ 90\frac{x_2}{x_2+x_5+x_8} + 105\frac{x_5}{x_2+x_5+x_8} + 110\frac{x_8}{x_2+x_5+x_8} & \geq & 97 \\ 90\frac{x_3}{x_3+x_6+x_9} + 105\frac{x_6}{x_3+x_6+x_9} + 110\frac{x_9}{x_3+x_6+x_9} & \geq & 105 \end{array} \right\} \text{ octane constraints}$$

$$\{ x_i \geq 0 \ (i = 1, 2, ..., 9) \} \text{ nonnegativity constraints}$$

We begin by inputing values for the parameters in cells C3 through E5 and in cells C8 through E10 (see Figure 3.6). Next, we use cells (E13 through E21 in our example) to hold the values of the variables x_1 through x_9. Based on the profit function P, we input the proper formula in cell C23. Then, in order to solve the optimization problem, we select Solver under the the menu option Tools. When the Solver Parameters window pops up, we select the desired input (see Figure 3.7).

In the solver window, we set the target cell C23 to a maximum by changing cells E13:E21. Next, we input our many requirements for a feasible solution. For example, the condition that we have only 10,000 barrels of component B available translates to the constraint

D28 >= E16+E17+E18.

As another example, the first octane constraint translates to

D33 <=
C3*(E13/(E13+E16+E19))+C4*(E16/(E13+E16+E19))+C5*(E19/(E14+E16+E19)).

The other required conditions (including the nonnegativity constraints) for this problem have been input into the spreadsheet for you. Finally, we hit Solve and let *Excel* do its work. *Excel* will output how we should use our resources to maximize our profit. Using these parameters, *Excel* will output that we should use 15,000 barrels

CHAPTER 3. LINEAR PROGRAMMING

of component A to make regular grade gasoline, 11,208 barrels of component A to make super grade gasoline, and 3,792 barrels of component A to make premium grade gasoline.

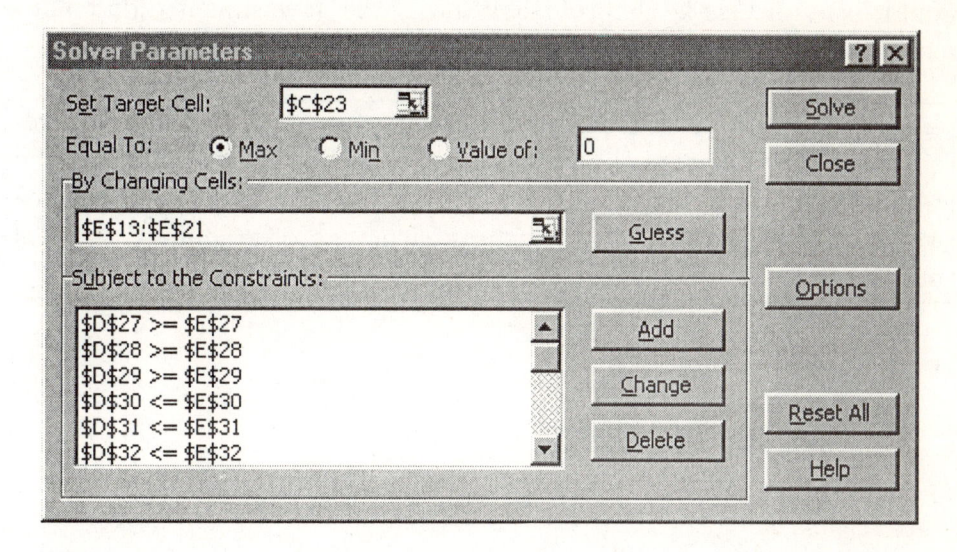

Figure 3.7: Using the `Solver` on the petroleum blending problem.

1. In the spreadsheet 'Petroleum Blending,' consider the formula in cell C23. Explain why it is that this is the formula we need to use to maximize profit.

2. Explain the reasoning behind the formula given in cell E27.

3. Explain the reasoning behind the formula given in cells E33 through E35.

4. How many barrels of super gasoline are produced at the optimal solution to the problem described above?

5. At the optimal solution, is the entire supply of component A used? If the price of component A were to be reduced to $29 per barrel, how would Gas-Iz-Us expect the optimal mix to change? How much more profit should Gas-Iz-Us expect to make with this $1 reduction per barrel cost of component A? Using the `Solver` in *Excel*, verify these facts. Can you draw any conclusions about what would happen if the price of component A were reduced to $20 per barrel?

6. At optimality, which constraints are binding? Does this suggest any actions Gas-Iz-Us should take to make more profit? That is, if they could increase the supply of any component by 1000 barrels, which component should they choose?

CHAPTER 3. LINEAR PROGRAMMING

7. Suppose the government were to pass a law requiring that premium gasoline *not* contain any of component A. By changing only cells E13:E14,E16:E21 within the Solver and setting cell E15 to a value of 0, describe the influence this law would have on Gas-Iz-Us profits. What if the government didn't allow super gasoline to contain any of component A either?

> **You make the call:** Suppose the government were to pass a law requiring that regular gasoline *not* contain any of component C. Describe the influence this law would have on profits. What, if any, influence would this law have on how much of each type of gasoline Gas-Iz-Us produces?

CHAPTER 3. LINEAR PROGRAMMING   63

3.3 Nonlinear Programming

[Download: NonlinearProject.xls]

Not all optimization problems involve only linear functions and equations. Often, the constraints and/or the objective function is not linear. Suppose, for example, we wish to find the point on the parabola $y = x^2$ closest to the ordered pair $(0.5, 2)$ as illustrated in Figure 3.8.

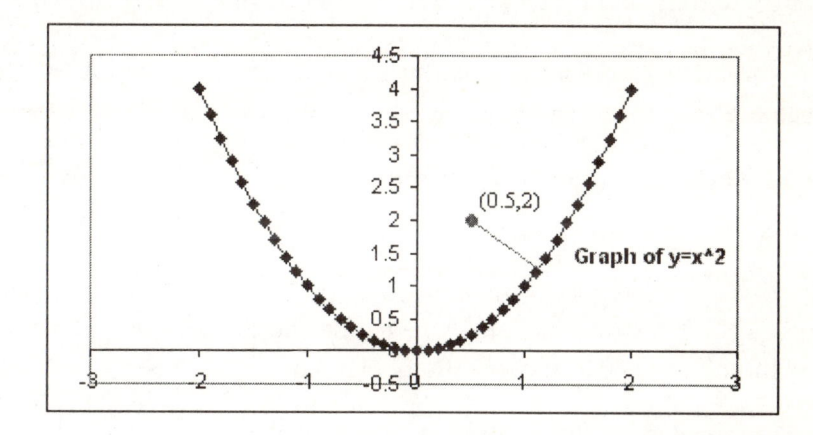

Figure 3.8: Minimizing the distance from $(0.5, 2)$ to the parabola $y = x^2$.

This optimization problem can be written as

$$\text{Minimize} \quad \sqrt{(x - 0.5)^2 + (y - 2)^2}$$
$$\text{subject to} \quad y - x^2 = 0$$

In this example, neither the constraint nor the objective function is linear. However, *Excel's* `Solver` can still give a solution to this problem.

	A	B	C	D	E	F
1	Minimize		0.86		x	1.300844
2					y	1.692195
3	Subject to		0.00			

Figure 3.9: Setting up the distance minimization problem for the `Solver`.

Figure 3.9 illustrates how to set this problem up for the `Solver`. To begin, we will place arbitrary values for x and y in cells `F1` and `F2` respectively. In cell `C1`, we place the formula

CHAPTER 3. LINEAR PROGRAMMING

```
=SQRT((F1-0.5)^2+(F2-2)^2)
```

which represents the quantity we would like to minimize. The value, =F2-F1^2, of the left hand side of the constraint is then placed in cell C3.

The final step in finding a solution to this problem is to choose the Solver under the Tools menu and enter the required information. In this example, we set the target cell C1 equal to a minimum by changing cells F1:F2 subject to the constraint C3=0. Upon solving, we find the minimum distance is approximately 0.8580 and it occurs at approximately the point (1.3, 1.7) as suggested by Figure 3.8.

1. Use the spreadsheet 'Distance to Parabola' to find the point on the parabola $y = x^2$ closest to the point $(0, 2)$

    (a) using an initial value of $x = 1$ and $y = 1$

    (b) using an initial value of $x = -1$ and $y = -1$

    Discuss any symmetry in your solutions by drawing a diagram such as that in Figure 3.8. What solution do you think the Solver would return using an initial value of $x = -0.5$ and $y = 0.25$? Explain.

2. Design your own spreadsheet which uses the Solver to find the point on the hyperbola $xy = 2$ closest to the origin. Can you find more than one solution to this problem? Draw a graph to help you decide.

You make the call: The Wee Widget company produces widgets. The average cost (in dollars) per widget of producing x widgets is given by

$$A(x) = \frac{1}{4}x + 4 + \frac{100}{x}.$$

Use the Solver in *Excel* to decide how many widgets this company should produce to minimize average cost per widget subject to the constraint that they produce one or more widgets. That is, solve the nonlinear optimization problem

$$\text{Minimize } \tfrac{1}{4}x + 4 + \tfrac{100}{x}$$
$$\text{subject to } \quad x \geq 1$$

What is the total cost of producing this many widgets?

CHAPTER 3. LINEAR PROGRAMMING 65

3.4 Linear Least Squares

[Download: LeastSquaresProject.xls]

In section 1.2.1, we used *Excel's* linear regression tools to find the best linear function to fit CPI data for the years 1987-1996. If x represented years since 1987, and $f(x)$ represented the value of the CPI, we saw that *Excel* found the best linear fit to be given by $f(x) = 4.8176x + 114.83$. How did *Excel* find this equation?

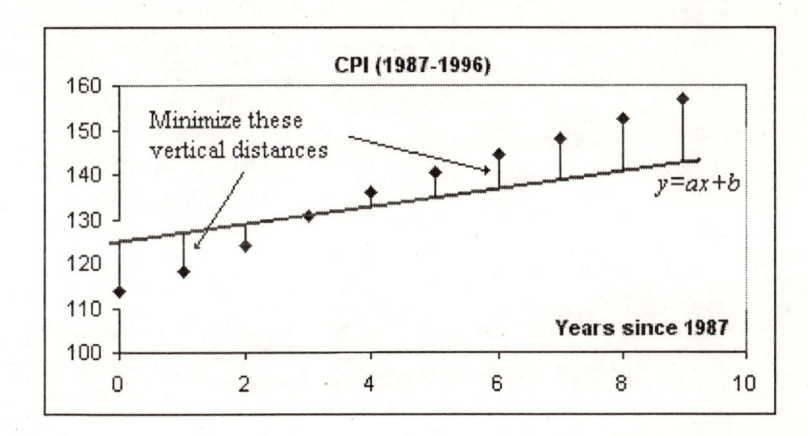

Figure 3.10: A graphical explanation of the least squares method.

The idea *Excel* uses in finding this equation is that of solving a minimization problem. What is the quantity being minimized? Distance. To be more precise, the sum of the squares of the vertical distances from each given ordered pair (x_i, y_i) to a variable line with equation $y = ax + b$ (see Figure 3.10). The precise minimization problem for the CPI data can be stated as

Minimize $(y_1 - ax_1 - b)^2 + (y_2 - ax_2 - b)^2 + \ldots + (y_{10} - ax_{10} - b)^2$
subject to
$$x_1 = 0, y_1 = 113.6$$
$$x_2 = 1, y_2 = 118.3$$
$$\vdots$$
$$x_{10} = 9, y_{10} = 156.9$$
a, b arbitrary

We can solve this (nonlinear!) minimization problem using *Excel's* `Solver`. First, as shown in Figure 3.11, we compute the values of $(y_i - ax_i - b)^2$ for each $1 \leq i \leq 10$. To do this, use the formula

=(D5-$B$2*B5-$D$2)^2

CHAPTER 3. LINEAR PROGRAMMING

containing a mixture of relative and absolute references in cell F5. Then, copy this formula down the next 9 cells in column F. In cell F16, we compute the sum of these squares using the formula =SUM(F5:F14). Our objective will be to minimize the value in this cell.

	A	B	C	D	E	F	G
1	Least Square Line: y=ax+b						
2	a	0	b	0			
3							
4	Ordered Pairs					(y_i-a*x_i-b)^2	
5	x1	0	y1	113.6		12904.96	
6	x2	1	y2	118.3		13994.89	
7	x3	2	y3	124		15376	
8	x4	3	y4	130.7		17082.49	
9	x5	4	y5	136.2		18550.44	
10	x6	5	y6	140.3		19684.09	
11	x7	6	y7	144.5		20880.25	
12	x8	7	y8	148.2		21963.24	
13	x9	8	y9	152.4		23225.76	
14	x10	9	y10	156.9		24617.61	
15							
16						188279.7	

Figure 3.11: Performing least squares on the CPI data.

Under the `Tools` menu, we start the `Solver`. Setting the target cell F16 equal to a minimum by changing cells B2 and D2 (entered as B2, D2), we let the `Solver` do its work. Notice the solution it produces. That's right! The `Solver` found the value of a in cell B2 to be 4.8176 and the value of b to be 114.83. This is exactly the same solution that *Excel's* linear regression tools produced.

1. Use the `Solver` tool in *Excel* to find the best linear fit to the 1987-2000 CPI data given in '1987-2000 CPI Data.' How does this compare to what *Excel's* linear regression tool gives?

2. Sometimes, we would like to weigh some data in a data set more than other data. For example, in our CPI example, the later years in the 1987-1996 data may be of more predictive value. So, rather than minimizing the sum of the squares of the vertical distances to a line $y = ax + b$, we might minimize a *weighted* sum of the squares of the vertical distances. The precise minimization

CHAPTER 3. LINEAR PROGRAMMING

problem might be stated as

$$\text{Minimize} \quad 1(y_1 - ax_1 - b)^2 + 2(y_2 - ax_2 - b)^2$$
$$+ 3(y_3 - ax_3 - b)^2 + \ldots + 10(y_{10} - ax_{10} - b)^2$$
$$\text{subject to} \quad x_1 = 0, y_1 = 113.6$$
$$x_2 = 1, y_2 = 118.3$$
$$\vdots$$
$$x_{10} = 9, y_{10} = 156.9$$
$$a, b \text{ arbitrary}$$

Use the Solver tool in *Excel* to find a weighted linear fit to the 1987-1996 CPI data as given in the spreadsheet 'Linear Least Squares.' When graphed on the actual data, your model should appear as in Figure 3.12.

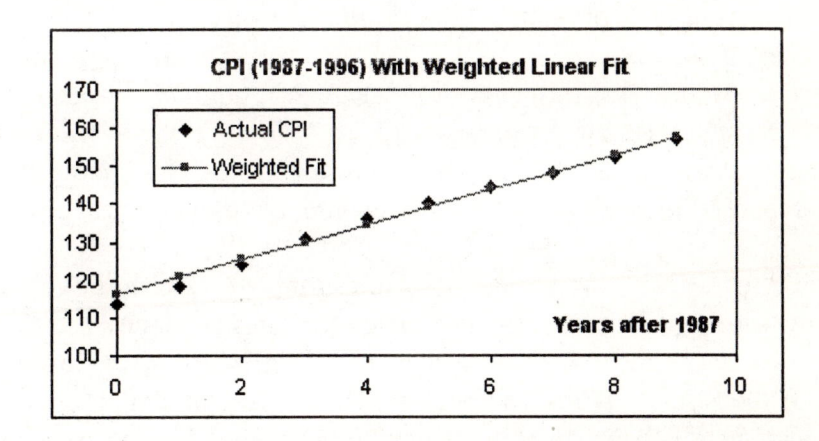

Figure 3.12: The result of a weighted least squares method.

> **You make the call:** Use the model $f(x) = 4.8176x + 114.83$ and the 'improved' model based on weighting the data found above to predict the 2000 CPI. If the actual 2000 CPI was 172.2, which model was a better predictor?

3.5 Portfolio Optimization: Markowitz's Quadratic Model

The Nobel Prize winning Markowitz portfolio selection model, proposed in 1952, is an optimization model for balancing the expected return and risk of a portfolio. Markowitz's model claimed that all the information needed to choose the best portfolio for any given level of risk is contained in three simple statistics: mean, standard deviation and correlation. This model fundamentally altered how investment decisions were made. While not completely relying upon it, virtually every major portfolio manager today consults an optimization program.

The Markowitz model uses the statistical variance of a stock's price as the measure of its risk. The decision variables are the amounts you invest in each asset. The objective is to minimize the overall variance of the portfolio's return, subject to the constraint that the expected return of the portfolio is greater than a specified amount. Just as linear programming problems, this **quadratic** programming problem can be solved using *Excel's* Solver.

Suppose we wish to invest in a mix of stock A and bond B. Stock A has had an average annual return of 12% and bond B a return of 5%. Our goal will be to have an average annual return of at least 10% while minimizing the risk involved. We let x_1 denote the percentage we will invest in stock A and x_2 the percentage we will invest in bond B.

The risk will be measured with a **covariance matrix** C. Without getting into the details, the covariance of two investments measures their tendency to vary together. If the two investments tend to increase together, then their **covariance** is greater than 0. If one investment tends to decrease when the other increases, then their covariance is less than 0. If the two investments are independent of one another, then their covariance is 0. Let us suppose that the covariance matrix for stock A and bond B is given by

$$\begin{pmatrix} 0.08 & -0.15 \\ -0.15 & 0.35 \end{pmatrix}.$$

The optimization problem that Markowitz proposes we solve is then given by

$$\begin{aligned} \text{Minimize} \quad & \begin{pmatrix} x_1 & x_2 \end{pmatrix} \begin{pmatrix} 0.08 & -0.15 \\ -0.15 & 0.35 \end{pmatrix} \begin{pmatrix} x_1 \\ x_2 \end{pmatrix} \\ \text{subject to} \quad & x_1 + x_2 = 1 \\ & 0.12 x_1 + 0.05 x_2 \geq 0.10 \\ & x_1 \geq 0, x_2 \geq 0 \end{aligned}$$

We can write this **nonlinear optimization problem** without using the matrix

CHAPTER 3. LINEAR PROGRAMMING

notation as

$$\text{Minimize} \quad 0.8x_1^2 - 0.30x_1x_2 + 0.35x_2^2$$
$$\text{subject to} \quad x_1 + x_2 = 1$$
$$0.12x_1 + 0.05x_2 \geq 0.10$$
$$x_1 \geq 0, x_2 \geq 0$$

	A	B	C	D	E	F	G	H	I
1	Cov C	0.08	-0.15		x1	0.714286			
2		-0.15	0.35		x2	0.285714			
3									
4	Return	x1	12.00%		Return	10.00%		x1	x2
5		x2	5.00%		Wanted			0.7143	0.2857
6									
7	Constraints				Minimize	0.008163			
8	1								
9	0.1								

Figure 3.13: Optimizing a portfolio by minimizing risk.

Using *Excel's* `Solver` tool to solve this problem is illustrated in Figure 3.13. The *formulas* for the constraints appear in cells `A8` and `A9`. In `A8`, we compute $x_1 + x_2$ using the formula `=F1+F2`. In `A9`, we compute $0.12x_1 + 0.05x_2$ using the formula `=F1*C4+F2*C5`. In order to compute the matrix product that we wish to minimize, we enter the formula

$$\texttt{=MMULT(MMULT(H5:I5,B1:C2),F1:F2)}$$

in cell `F7`.

After assigning cells `F1` and `F2` initial values such as 0.5 and 0.5, we proceed to choose the `Solver` from the `Tools` menu. We then enter the information as shown in Figure 3.14. The result, as shown in Figure 3.13 is that we should invest about 71.4% in stock A and about 28.6% in bond B. The value of 0.10 in cell `A9` tells us that the constraint regarding a 10% minimum return is binding and suggests that we could further minimize our risk by lowering our expectation of return.

1. Using the spreadsheet 'Markowitz Example,' determine how much we should invest in stock A and bond B above if we only require a return of 9.5%. Compared to the solution for a required 10% return, does the answer make sense? Can we minimize our risk even more by requiring only 9% return? 8%?

CHAPTER 3. LINEAR PROGRAMMING   70

2. How do you think we will need to allocate our money in a portfolio containing stock A and bond B if we require a return of 11.95%? Does the solution to this problem given by the `Solver` make sense?

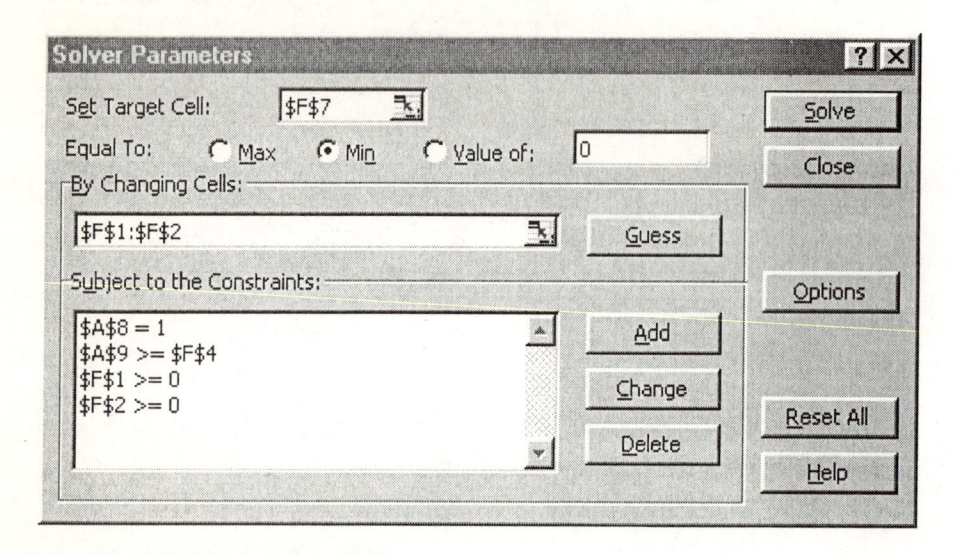

Figure 3.14: Using the `Solver` to minimize risk.

CHAPTER 3. LINEAR PROGRAMMING

> **You make the call:** Suppose that you would like to form an investment portfolio consisting of three stocks with expected returns of 5%, 11%, and 8% respectively and a covariance matrix given by
>
> $$C = \begin{pmatrix} 0.00044 & 0.00042 & 0.00015 \\ 0.00042 & 0.02341 & 0.00458 \\ 0.00015 & 0.00458 & 0.00774 \end{pmatrix}.$$
>
> If you require a minimal return of 6.5% on this portfolio, use the spreadsheet 'Three Stocks' to decide how much of your portfolio should be allocated to each stock in order to minimize risk. That is, use *Excel's* Solver to solve the optimization problem
>
> $$\text{Minimize} \quad \begin{pmatrix} x_1 & x_2 & x_3 \end{pmatrix} \begin{pmatrix} 0.00044 & 0.00042 & 0.00015 \\ 0.00042 & 0.02341 & 0.00458 \\ 0.00015 & 0.00458 & 0.00774 \end{pmatrix} \begin{pmatrix} x_1 \\ x_2 \\ x_3 \end{pmatrix}$$
>
> subject to
> $$x_1 + x_2 + x_3 = 1$$
> $$0.05 x_1 + 0.11 x_2 + 0.08 x_3 \geq 0.065$$
> $$x_1 \geq 0, x_2 \geq 0, x_3 \geq 0$$
>
> How do you expect this investment mix to change if you require a minimal return of 7.5%? Does the investment mix indeed change in this fashion?

3.6 Appendix

To add Excel's `Solver` to your `Tools` menu:

- Select the menu option `Tools | Add Ins` (this will take a few moments to load the necessary file).

- From the dialogue box presented check the box for `Solver Add-In`.

- On clicking OK, you will then be able to access the `Solver` option from the new menu option `Tools | Solver` (which appears below `Tools | Scenarios` ...)

Chapter 4

The Simplex Method

In this chapter, we will use spreadsheets to take much of the computational pain out of applying the **simplex method**. This will allow us to concentrate on *how* to make better decisions about how to best use the information that the simplex method gives us. Often, we are not as interested in what an optimal solution is, but rather what steps should be taken to make the optimal solution even better.

4.1 Finite Mathematics Tutoring

[Download: FiniteTutoringProject.xls]

Alas, it is apparent that Felicia only has a finite amount of time to do Finite Mathematics tutoring. Further complicating matters, Felicia's clients (Alphie, Beta, and Celina) only have a finite amount of money to pay her. We will illustrate how the spreadsheet can help Felicia maximize her Finite tutoring income.

Let us suppose that Alphie has negotiated to pay $10 per hour (for up to 30 hours per month) for Finite Math tutoring, Beta will pay $12 per hour (up to 25 hours) for tutoring, and Celina will pay $16 per hour (up to 20 hours) for tutoring. We will assume that Felicia has only 40 hours per month of her own time available for tutoring. Lastly, we will assume that Felicia has to travel to meet with her clients. She must travel 1/10 of an hour for every one hour session with Alphie and must travel 2/10 of an hour for every hour session with either Beta or Celina. We assume that Felicia only has 24 hours of travel time available per month.

If x_i ($i = 1, 2, 3$) is the number of hours per month devoted to tutoring for Alicia,

CHAPTER 4. THE SIMPLEX METHOD

Beta, and Celina respectively, we can write this optimization problem in the form

$$\text{Maximize} \quad z = 10x_1 + 12x_2 + 16x_3$$
$$\text{subject to} \quad x_1 + x_2 + x_3 \leq 40$$
$$0.1x_1 + 0.2x_2 + 0.2x_3 \leq 24$$
$$x_1 \leq 30$$
$$x_2 \leq 25$$
$$x_3 \leq 20$$
$$x_1, x_2, x_3 \geq 0$$

The initial simplex tableau for this problem is shown in Figure 4.1. The bottom row of the tableau contains the coefficents of the objective function. The other rows in the tableau show the coefficents of the constraints in the variables x_1, x_2, x_3 and the slack variables s_1, s_2, s_3, s_4, s_5. By using the information provided (verify this information by hand!) in columns L and M, it is clear that we are to pivot on the value 1 in cell C7. That is, x_3 will become a basic variable and slack variable s_5 will become a nonbasic variable.

	A	B	C	D	E	F	G	H	I	J	K	L	M
1	X1	X2	X3	S1	S2	S3	S4	S5	Z	RHS			Ratio
2													
3	1	1	1	1	0	0	0	0	0	40		Pivot Column	40
4	0.1	0.2	0.2	0	1	0	0	0	0	24		3	120
5	1	0	0	0	0	1	0	0	0	30			undefined
6	0	1	0	0	0	0	1	0	0	25			undefined
7	0	0	1	0	0	0	0	1	0	20			20
8	-10	-12	-16	0	0	0	0	0	1	0			

Figure 4.1: The initial simplex tableau for Felicia's tutoring problem.

By using the spreadsheet 'Finite Tutoring,' we can pivot on the element in cell C7. The results of this pivoting operation are shown in Figure 4.2.

1. Does the second simplex tableau yield an optimal solution to Felicia's tutoring problem? Explain.

2. Based on the output of Figure 4.2, which element should be the pivot element in the second simplex tableau?

3. Use the spreadsheet 'Finite Tutoring' to continue pivoting, if necessary, until an optimal solution is reached. What is Felica's maximal monthly profit from tutoring? How can she reach that amount?

4. The '12' in the objective row of the final simplex tableau is in the column corresponding to slack variable s_1. This number means that Felicia could increase her profit by $12 per month if she could add one additional hour of tutoring to her schedule (i.e. the first constraint regarding the 40 hours Felicia has available each month is binding). What do you think the '4' in the objective row of the final simplex tableau (under the column heading s_5) means? Should Felica put pressure on Celina to buy more hours of tutoring?

	A	B	C	D	E	F	G	H	I	J	K	L	M
1	X1	X2	X3	S1	S2	S3	S4	S5	Z	RHS			Ratio
2													
3	1	1	1	1	0	0	0	0	0	40		Pivot Column	40
4	0.1	0.2	0.2	0	1	0	0	0	0	24		3	120
5	1	0	0	0	0	1	0	0	0	30			undefined
6	0	1	0	0	0	0	1	0	0	25			undefined
7	0	0	1	0	0	0	0	1	0	20			20
8	-10	-12	-16	0	0	0	0	0	1	0			
9													
10	1	1	0	1	0	0	0	-1	0	20		Pivot Column	20
11	0.1	0.2	0	0	1	0	0	-0.2	0	20		2	100
12	1	0	0	0	0	1	0	0	0	30			undefined
13	0	1	0	0	0	0	1	0	0	25			25
14	0	0	1	0	0	0	0	1	0	20			undefined
15	-10	-12	0	0	0	0	0	16	1	320			

Figure 4.2: The first and second simplex tableau for Felicia's tutoring problem.

5. Working 40 hours a month, Felicia's optimal solution tells her to work with Beta for 20 hours (at $12 an hour) and with Celina for 20 hours (at $16 an hour). Common sense suggests that if Felicia increases the number she is willing to work to 45, she should work with Beta for 25 hours and with Celina for 20 hours. Run the simplex method with this new constraint in the spreadsheet 'Finite Tutoring' to determine if the mathematics also suggests this approach. What do you expect the solution to be if Felicia is willing to work for 50 hours a month? Verify this on the spreadsheet.

6. Suppose that Alphie, not getting any of Felicia's tutoring services, were to offer to pay Felicia $14 an hour (for up to 30 hours). Using common sense, describe how Felicia would change her behavior. Verify that the common sense solution to this new optimization problem is also the solution that the simplex method gives using the spreadsheet 'Finite Tutoring.'

> **You make the call:** Suppose that Celina wishes to increase her amount of tutoring from 20 to 25 hours per month. What does common sense suggest that Felicia's allocation of her 40 monthly hours should be? How much more profit should Felicia expect to make? Verify that the common sense solution to this new optimization problem is also the solution that the simplex method gives by using the spreadsheet 'Finite Tutoring.'

4.2 Curing Math Phobia

[Download: MathPhobiaProject.xls]

A pharmaceutical company has developed a cure for math phobia. The first product, called "Simplex-Gone," is intended for business majors required to take mathematics courses. The second product, called "Count-EZ," is intended for a more general audience. Every bottle of Simplex-Gone returns a profit of $0.25 and every bottle of Count-EZ returns a profit of $0.15.

These new products can only be produced during FiniteFest – an annual summer ritual for professional mathematicians. It follows that the total amount produced must fit within a specially designed (imagine the shape!) warehouse which has a current capacity of 200,000 cubic inches. Each bottle consumes 1 cubic inch of warehouse space.

Production rates are 4,000 and 5,000 bottles per hour for Simplex-Gone and Count-EZ, respectively, with a total of 65 hours per year available for production.

By law, the maximum yearly amounts that can be sold are 125,000 bottles of Simplex-Gone and 175,000 bottles of Count-EZ. Due to a contract signed during development, the pharmaceutical company must also provide 25,000 bottles per year of Count-EZ to the Ivy League universities.

If x_1 denotes the number of bottles of Simplex-Gone produced each year and x_2 denotes the number of bottles of Count-EZ produced each year, we can formulate the optimization problem as shown below.

$$\begin{aligned}
\text{Maximize} \quad & z = 0.25x_1 + 0.15x_2 \\
\text{subject to} \quad & x_1 + x_2 \leq 200{,}000 \\
& \tfrac{1}{4{,}000}x_1 + \tfrac{1}{5000}x_2 \leq 65 \\
& x_1 \leq 125{,}000 \\
& x_2 \leq 175{,}000 \\
& x_2 \geq 25{,}000 \\
& x_1, x_2 \geq 0
\end{aligned}$$

Before we can begin to use the simplex method, we must put the problem in standard maximization form. For this, we will use the two-phase process. Since the last constraint is $-x_2 \leq -25{,}000$, the initial simplex tableau is as shown in Figure 4.3.

CHAPTER 4. THE SIMPLEX METHOD

	A	B	C	D	E	F	G	H	I
1	X1	X2	S1	S2	S3	S4	S5	Z	RHS
2									
3	1	1	1	0	0	0	0	0	200000
4	0.0003	0.0002	0	1	0	0	0	0	65
5	1	0	0	0	1	0	0	0	125000
6	0	1	0	0	0	1	0	0	175000
7	0	-1	0	0	0	0	1	0	-25000
8	-0.25	-0.15	0	0	0	0	0	1	0

Figure 4.3: Initial simplex tableau for the Math Phobia problem.

Since the initial solution is not feasible, we begin by pivoting on the value -1 in cell B7 of the spreadsheet 'Curing Math Phobia.' The result is shown in Figure 4.4. Notice that since the rightmost column in the second tableau is all nonnegative, we can proceed.

	A	B	C	D	E	F	G	H	I	J	K	L
1	X1	X2	S1	S2	S3	S4	S5	Z	RHS			Ratio
2												
3	1	1	1	0	0	0	0	0	200000			
4	0.0003	0.0002	0	1	0	0	0	0	65			
5	1	0	0	0	1	0	0	0	125000			
6	0	1	0	0	0	1	0	0	175000			
7	0	-1	0	0	0	0	1	0	-25000			
8	-0.25	-0.15	0	0	0	0	0	1	0			
9												
10	1	0	1	0	0	0	1	0	175000		Pivot Column	175000
11	0.0003	0	0	1	0	0	0.0002	0	60		1	240000
12	1	0	0	0	1	0	0	0	125000			125000
13	0	0	0	0	0	1	1	0	150000			undefined
14	0	1	0	0	0	0	-1	0	25000			undefined
15	-0.25	0	0	0	0	0	-0.15	1	3750			

Figure 4.4: First and second simplex tableau for the Math Phobia problem.

1. Based on the output of Figure 4.4, which element should be the pivot element in the second simplex tableau?

2. Use the spreadsheet 'Curing Math Phobia' to find the optimal solution for the Math Phobia problem. How much Simplex-Gone and Count-EZ should be produced? What is the maximal profit?

CHAPTER 4. THE SIMPLEX METHOD

3. The '0.15' in the objective row of the final simplex tableau is in the column corresponding to slack variable s_1. This number means that the pharmaceutical company can increase profit by \$0.15 per year if they could add one additional cubic inch of warehouse space (i.e. the first constraint regarding yearly warehouse capacity is binding). What do you think the '0.1' in the objective row of the final simplex tableau (under the column heading s_3) means? Should the company lobby to change the law restricting sales of Simplex-Gone? Should they lobby as hard to change the law restricting sales of Count-EZ?

4. Suppose that a grass roots movement changes the restriction on yearly sales of Simplex-Gone from 125,000 bottles to 150,000 bottles. How many bottles of each Math phobia product should be produced?

5. If the law restricting sales of Simplex-Gone to 125,000 bottles per year was abolished altogether, how much more profit would the pharmaceutical company stand to gain each year?

> **You make the call:** Suppose that mathematicians have found a way to expand the warehouse for Simplex-Gone and Count-EZ to 300,000 cubic inches. Use the spreadsheet 'Curing Math Phobia' to determine the binding constraints at the optimal solution. Do you have any sage advice to give the company?

4.3 Feeding the Survivors

[Download: SurvivorProject.xls]

A game show in which several people are left to fend for themselves on a deserted island for six weeks would like to construct a special diet using foods A, B, and C. Figure 4.5 gives the nutritional contents of each food.

	Units per Ounce		
	A	B	C
Calcium	30	10	30
Iron	10	10	10
Vitamin C	10	30	20
Fat	2.4	1.2	1.8
Calories	60	40	50

Figure 4.5: Nutritional information for the survival game show.

The objective of the creators of the show is to feed the survivalists amounts of these three foods in such a way that each person receives a required minimum daily allowance of calcium, iron, and Vitamin C (400, 200, and 300 units respectively), a required maximum daily allowance of 45 units of fat, and in such a way that the number of calories each survivalists receives is minimized. If x_i ($i = 1, 2, 3$) denotes the number of ounces of each food (A, B, and C respectively) each survivalists is to receive each day, the optimization problem can be stated as shown below.

$$\begin{aligned}
\text{Minimize} \quad & 60x_1 + 40x_2 + 50x_3 \\
\text{subject to} \quad & 30x_1 + 10x_2 + 30x_3 \geq 400 \\
& 10x_1 + 10x_2 + 10x_3 \geq 200 \\
& 10x_1 + 30x_2 + 20x_3 \geq 300 \\
& 2.4x_1 + 1.2x_2 + 1.8x_3 \leq 45 \\
& x_1, x_2, x_3 \geq 0
\end{aligned}$$

We can convert this problem to a dual maximization problem very easily.

$$\begin{aligned}
\text{Maximize} \quad & 400y_1 + 200y_2 + 300y_3 - 45y_4 \\
\text{subject to} \quad & 30y_1 + 10y_2 + 10y_3 - 2.4y_4 \leq 60 \\
& 10y_1 + 10y_2 + 30y_3 - 1.2y_4 \leq 40 \\
& 30y_1 + 10y_2 + 20y_3 - 1.8y_4 \leq 50 \\
& y_1, y_2, y_3, y_4 \geq 0
\end{aligned}$$

CHAPTER 4. THE SIMPLEX METHOD

The initial simplex tableau for the dual problem is shown in Figure 4.6. Note that we can still perform the simplex method on this tableau even though the objective row contains a positive value.

Y1	Y2	Y3	Y4	S1	S2	S3	Z	RHS
30	10	10	-2.4	1	0	0	0	60
10	10	30	-1.2	0	1	0	0	40
30	10	20	-1.8	0	0	1	0	50
-400	-200	-300	45	0	0	0	1	0

Figure 4.6: The initial simplex tableau in the survivalist problem.

1. Determine the pivot element for the initial simplex tableau in the dual survivalist problem. Then, use the spreadsheet 'Survivor!' to find the optimal solution to the dual maximization problem. What are the values of y_1, y_2, y_3, and y_4 at the optimal solution?

2. The **Fundamental Principle of Duality** states that the optimal value of the minimization problem is the same as the optimal value of the dual (maximization) problem. According to the output of the previous problem, what is the minimum number of calories that the creators of the show should feed the survivalists?

3. The optimal solution to the initial minimization problem can always be obtained by looking at the bottom (objective) row of final tableau in the dual problem. How? The slack variables s_1, s_2, and s_3 in the dual correspond to the variables x_1, x_2, and x_3 in the original minimization problem. Thus, at optimality, we have $x_1 = 0$ and $x_2 = 10$. How many ounces of food C should be given to each survivalist per day?

4. In an attempt to give the survivalists a more diversified diet, the creators (seeing that food A was not part of the previous solution) decide to replace food A with an alternative food A' containing 45 calories, 25 units of calcium, 10 units of iron, 15 units of vitamin C, and 2.0 units of fat per ounce. Make these changes to the initial tableau (as shown in Figure 4.6), perform the simplex method using the power of the spreadsheet, and interpret the results. If "fewer calories=better ratings," should the creators use this new diet consisting of foods A', B, and C?

> **You make the call:** Could the fashion in which the simplex method is implemented affect the survivalists diet? Suppose that food A is replaced with an alternative food A″ containing 45 calories, 20 units of calcium, 10 units of iron, 20 units of vitamin C, and 1.6 units of fat per ounce. Make these changes to the initial tableau and perform the simplex method using the spreadsheet 'Survivor!.' If any tie occurs in choosing a pivot element, does the way you break that tie affect the optimal diet to be provided? Which diet might yield better TV ratings?

CHAPTER 4. THE SIMPLEX METHOD

4.4 Bubble Head Dolls

[Download: BubbleHeadProject.xls]

One of the latest gimmicks to bring people into a sporting event has been the "Bubble Head Doll" night. These items, made in very limited quantity, have been known to sell on eboy.com for very large sums of money.

The Blow Hard Bubbles company produces these Bubble Head dolls in two plants. The company's contract enables them to sell every doll they produce. Plant A can produce a total of 3000 Bubble Head dolls each month. They can produce Mork McHire dolls for a profit of $1.50 each. They can also produce Sunny Soso dolls for a profit of $2.00 each. Plant B can produce a total of 2000 Bubble Head dolls each month. They can produce Mork McHire dolls for a profit of $1.35 each and Sunny Soso dolls for a profit of $1.80 each. According to its contract, the Blow Hard Bubbles company will limit production to 2500 Mork McHire dolls and 2000 Sunny Soso dolls each month.

If x_1 and x_3 represent the number of Mork McHire dolls produced at plants A and B respectively and x_2 and x_4 represent the number of Sunny Soso dolls produced at plants A and B respectively, then we can formulate the optimization problem as follows.

$$\begin{aligned} \text{Maximize} \quad & 1.5x_1 + 2.0x_2 + 1.35x_3 + 1.8x_4 \\ \text{subject to} \quad & x_1 + x_2 \leq 3000 \\ & x_3 + x_4 \leq 2000 \\ & x_1 + x_3 = 2500 \\ & x_2 + x_4 = 2000 \\ & x_1, x_2, x_3, x_4 \geq 0 \end{aligned}$$

Using the "Big M" method, we can use surplus and artificial variables to rewrite this problem in the following form where M is a large (relatively speaking) positive number.

$$\begin{aligned} \text{Maximize} \quad & 1.5x_1 + 2.0x_2 + 1.35x_3 + 1.8x_4 - Ma_1 - Ma_2 \\ \text{subject to} \quad & x_1 + x_2 + s_1 = 3000 \\ & x_3 + x_4 + s_2 = 2000 \\ & x_1 + x_3 + a_1 = 2500 \\ & x_2 + x_4 + a_2 = 2000 \\ & x_1, x_2, x_3, x_4, s_1, s_2, a_1, a_2 \geq 0 \end{aligned}$$

CHAPTER 4. THE SIMPLEX METHOD 84

The first simplex tableau for this problem in standard form using $M = 1000$ is shown in Figure 4.7.

X1	X2	X3	X4	S1	S2	A1	A2	Z	RHS		Ratio
1	1	0	0	1	0	0	0	0	3000	Pivot Column	3000
0	0	1	1	0	1	0	0	0	2000		2 undefined
1	0	1	0	0	0	1	0	0	2500		undefined
0	1	0	1	0	0	0	1	0	2000		2000
-1.5	-2	-1.35	-1.8	0	0	1000	1000	1	0		

Figure 4.7: The initial simplex tableau for the Bubble Head Doll problem.

1. Based on the output of Figure 4.7, which element should be the pivot element in the first simplex tableau?

2. Use the spreadsheet 'Bubble Heads' to determine the optimal solution to the problem described above. What is the maximum profit the Blow Hard Bubbles company can make? What does it mean to have $s_2 = 500$ at optimality in this problem?

3. Do the values of $M > 0$ matter in this problem? Experiment with various values of $M > 0$. Why can't we use $M = -2$? What happens in general when $M < -2$?

4. Use the spreadsheet 'Unrestricted Bubble Heads' to determine the outcome of not restricting production to 2500 Mork McHire and 2000 Sunny Soso dolls each month. How much profit can the Blow Hard Bubbles company make?

> **You make the call:** Considering the contractual restriction of producing a maximum of 2500 Mork McHire and 2000 Sunny Soso dolls each month, use the final tableau in the spreadsheet 'Bubble Heads' to determine which plant is holding the Blow Hard Bubbles company back from making more profit each month?

CHAPTER 4. THE SIMPLEX METHOD

4.5 Which Optimal Solution?

[Download: ChoosingPivotProject.xls]

Does the simplex method always yield the same optimal solution? If our goal, for example, is to decide how many square widgets x_1 to produce and how many round widgets x_2 to produce to maximize profit, will we arrive at the same answer regardless of how ties are broken in the simplex method?

To answer this question, we will consider several examples.

1. First, consider the linear programming problem[1]

$$\begin{aligned} \text{Maximize} \quad & z = x_1 + x_2 \\ \text{subject to} \quad & 2x_1 + x_2 \leq 16 \\ & x_1 \leq 6 \\ & x_2 \leq 10 \\ & x_1, x_2 \geq 0 \end{aligned}$$

   (a) Using the spreadsheet 'Example 1,' begin by choosing column 1 as the pivot column. What are the optimal values of x_1 and x_2? What is the value of the objective function z at the optimal solution?

   (b) Using the spreadsheet 'Example 2,' begin the simplex method now by choosing column 2 as the pivot column. Do you arrive at the same optimal values of x_1 and x_2? Is the value of the objective function z at this optimal solution the same or different?

   (c) Using the graph of the feasible region shown in Figure 4.8, describe the path that the basic solution in the simplex method followed in each of the two cases above.

---

[1] From *Finite Mathematics for Business, Economics, Life Sciences, and Social Sciences* (8th ed.) by Barnett, Ziegler, and Byleen.

CHAPTER 4. THE SIMPLEX METHOD							86

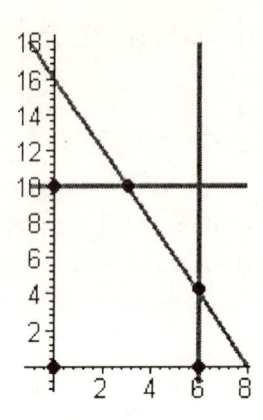

Figure 4.8: Feasible region for optimization problem 1.

2. Next, consider the similar linear programming problem

$$\begin{aligned} \text{Maximize} \quad & z = x_1 + x_2 \\ \text{subject to} \quad & x_1 + 2x_2 \leq 10 \\ & x_1 \leq 6 \\ & x_2 \leq 4 \\ & x_1, x_2 \geq 0 \end{aligned}$$

(a) Using the spreadsheet 'Example 3,' begin by choosing column 1 as the pivot column. What are the optimal values of x_1 and x_2? What is the value of the objective function z at the optimal solution?

(b) Using the spreadsheet 'Example 4,' begin the simplex method now by choosing column 2 as the pivot column. Do you arrive at the same optimal values of x_1 and x_2? Is the value of the objective function z at this optimal solution the same or different?

(c) Using the graph of the feasible region shown in Figure 4.9, describe the path that the basic solution in the simplex method followed in each of the two cases above.

CHAPTER 4. THE SIMPLEX METHOD

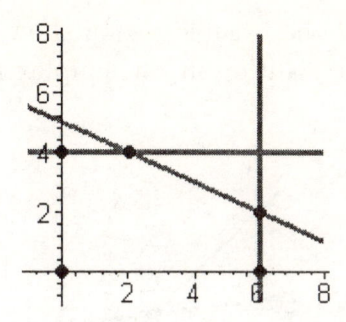

Figure 4.9: Feasible region for optimization problem 2.

3. Consider now the linear programming problem

$$\begin{aligned}\text{Maximize} \quad & 3x_1 + 3x_2 + 2x_3 \\ \text{subject to} \quad & x_1 + x_2 + 2x_3 \leq 20 \\ & 2x_1 + x_2 + 4x_3 \leq 32 \\ & x_1, x_2, x_3 \geq 0\end{aligned}$$

(a) Using the spreadsheet 'Example 5,' begin by choosing column 1 as the pivot column. What are the optimal values of x_1 and x_2? What is the value of the objective function z at the optimal solution?

(b) Using the spreadsheet 'Example 6,' begin the simplex method now by choosing column 2 as the pivot column. Do you arrive at the same optimal values of x_1 and x_2? Is the value of the objective function z at this optimal solution the same or different?

4. Consider the linear problemming problem

$$\begin{aligned}\text{Maximize} \quad & 3x_1 + 12x_2 \\ \text{subject to} \quad & 2x_1 + x_2 \leq 120 \\ & x_1 + 4x_2 \leq 200 \\ & x_1, x_2 \geq 0\end{aligned}$$

(a) Using the spreadsheet 'Example 7,' determine the optimal values of x_1 and x_2. What is the value of the objective function z at the optimal solution?

(b) Continuing with the simplex method on the spreadsheet 'Example 7,' make x_1 a basic variable by pivoting on the element 1.75 in cell **A7**. What optimal values of x_1 and x_2 do you arrive at? Is the value of the objective function z at *this* optimal solution the same or different?

(c) Using the graph of the feasible region shown in Figure 4.10, describe the path that the basic solution in the simplex method followed in the above exercises.

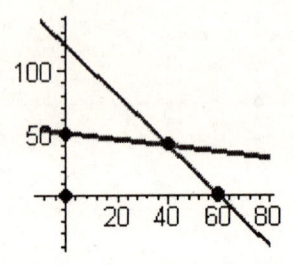

Figure 4.10: Feasible region for optimization problem 4.

> **You make the call:** Wiggly Wigets produces two types of widgets - round and square. Round widgets require 1 hour in the cutting department and 1 hour in the gluing department. Square widgets require 1/2 hour in the cutting department and 1 hour in the gluing department. The Wiggly Wigets factory has 16 hours/day available in the cutting department and 24 hours/day available in the gluing department. Round widgets sell for $2 each and square widgets sell for $1 each.
>
> One analyst for the company, Joe Leftoe, claims you should make 16 round widgets and 0 square widgets every day in order to maximize profit. Another company analyst, Jeff Leftoe, claims you should make 8 round widgets and 16 square widgets each day to maximize profit. After one step of the simplex method, your boss determines that Joe must be right and fires Jeff. Use the spreadsheet 'You Make The Call' to show your boss that Jeff's solution was just as good. Attempt to argue to your boss that Jeff's solution was even better.

4.6 Cycling

[Download: BealesProject.xls]

Sometimes, the simplex method simply fails. That is, we can choose all the right pivot elements, perform all the required calculations to perfection and still fail to reach an optimal solution.[2] The smallest known case, due to E. Beale is illustrated in this project.

Consider the linear programming problem[3]

$$\text{Maximize} \quad -0.75x_1 + 150x_2 - 0.02x_3 + 6x_4$$
$$\text{subject to} \quad 0.25x_1 - 60x_2 - 0.04x_3 + 9x_4 \leq 0$$
$$0.5x_1 - 90x_2 - 0.02x_3 + 3x_4 \leq 0$$
$$x_3 \leq 1$$
$$x_i \geq 0 \qquad (i = 1, 2, 3, 4)$$

The initial tableau for this linear programming problem is shown in Figure 4.11. The bottom row of the tableau contains the coefficents of the objective function. The other rows in the tableau show the coefficents of the constraints in the variables x_1, x_2, x_3, x_4 and the slack variables s_1, s_2, s_3.

X1	X2	X3	X4	S1	S2	S3	Z	RHS
0.25	-60	-0.04	9	1	0	0	0	0
0.5	-90	-0.02	3	0	1	0	0	0
0	0	1	0	0	0	1	0	1
-0.75	150	-0.02	6	0	0	0	1	0

Figure 4.11: The initial simplex tableau for E. Beale's example.

In performing the simplex method on this tableau, we have some choices as to the pivot elements. For example at the first step, we could choose to pivot on either the value 0.25 in cell A3 or on the value 0.5 in cell A4. Suppose for the moment we decide to initially pivot on the value 0.25 in cell A3. To do this, we can simply select cell A3 in the spreadsheet 'Beale's Example' and click on the button which performs the required pivot operation.

In the second tableau, it is clear that column 2 is the pivot column. Furthermore, this column has a clear choice for the pivot element. We pivot on the value 30 in cell B9. At this point, the spreadsheet will appear as in Figure 4.12.

---

[2] To learn how to avoid this rare problem, investigate a method called *Bland's rule*.
[3] From *An Example of Cycling in the Simplex Method* by Harvey Greenberg.

CHAPTER 4. THE SIMPLEX METHOD 90

X1	X2	X3	X4	S1	S2	S3	Z	RHS
0.25	-60	-0.04	9	1	0	0	0	0
0.5	-90	-0.02	3	0	1	0	0	0
0	0	1	0	0	0	1	0	1
-0.75	150	-0.02	6	0	0	0	1	0
1	-240	-0.16	36	4	0	0	0	0
0	30	0.06	-15	-2	1	0	0	0
0	0	1	0	0	0	1	0	1
0	-30	-0.14	33	3	0	0	1	0

Figure 4.12: The first two tableau in the simplex method for E. Beale's example.

The third tableau gives us yet another choice as to how we may proceed. While column 3 is clearly the pivot column, we could pivot on either element in the first or second row. Let us decide, perhaps by a coin flip, to pivot on the value 0.32 in cell C13.

In the fourth tableau, our hands are tied and we must pivot on the value 0.025 in cell D19. The fifth tableau presents a choice in pivot element to us once again. Suppose that we pivot on the value 50 in cell E23. In tableau six, we are forced to pivot on the value 1/3 in cell F29.

Do you notice anything familiar about the seventh tableau? That's right...it *is* *exactly* the first tableau! This phenomenon is called **cycling** in the simplex method.

> **You make the call:** Does cycling always occur in Beale's example? That is, did the choices we made for pivot elements cause the cycling or would the simplex method have converged to an optimal solution by choosing different (yet legal!) pivot elements? For starters, you might try pivoting on the value 0.5 in cell A5.

Chapter 5

The Mathematics of Finance

5.1 Building Custom Financial Calculators

[Download: CalculatorProject.xls]

One valuable use of the modern spreadsheet is that of making custom financial calculators. In financial mathematics, formulas abound and the spreadsheet can help to take some of the pain out of applying these. Of course, it will always be necessary to *understand* how to apply these formulas to the correct situations. But, thankfully, modern technology has lessened the need to be a computational whiz.

	A
1	Initial amount in savings account
2	$2,000.00
3	
4	Interest rate r
5	7.00%
6	
7	Compounding periods per year k
8	12
9	
10	Number of years passed N
11	2
12	
13	Amount in account after N years
14	$2,299.61

Figure 5.1: A calculator which directly applies the compound interest formula.

To illustrate the idea, we build a calculator that will directly apply the compound

interest formula
$$A_N = A_0 \left(1 + \frac{r}{k}\right)^{kN}$$
where A_N is the amount in an account after N years with an initial amount A_0 invested at an interest rate r compounded k times a year. Consider the 'compound interest calculator' developed in the spreadsheet 'Compound Interest Savings' shown in Figure 5.1. The key formula is

```
=A2*(1+A5/A8)^(A8*A11)
```

which occurs in cell A14. The beauty behind this calculator is that the user can change any of the values in cells A2, A5, A8, or A11 and the output in cell A14 will update automatically and quickly. Also, as we will see in the next project, we can seek (using Goal Seek) a particular input which gives a desired output.

	A
1	Period Payment PMT
2	$100.00
3	
4	Interest rate per period I
5	0.50%
6	
7	Number of payments (periods) n
8	12
9	
10	Future Value FV
11	$1,233.56

Figure 5.2: A calculator which directly applies the future value of an annuity formula.

As another example, Figure 5.2 illustrates a 'future value of an annuity calculator' that can be found in the spreadsheet 'Future Value of Annuity.' You may recall that the future value of an annuity is given by
$$FV = PMT \frac{(1+i)^n - 1}{i}$$
where FV is the future value of an ordinary annuity at a periodic interest rate i in which n equal periodic payments PMT are made at the end of each time interval. The key formula in this calculator,

```
=A2*((1+A5)^A8-1)/A5,
```

CHAPTER 5. THE MATHEMATICS OF FINANCE

occurs in cell A11.[1]

1. In the workbook CalculatorProject.xls, consider the spreadsheet 'No Interest Savings.' Turn this spreadsheet into a calculator which allows the user to vary the values in cells A2, A5, and A8 and outputs the value of an account receiving regular deposits but accruing no interest to cell A11 by entering an appropriate formula in that cell.

2. Consider the spreadsheet 'Annually Compounded Savings' in the workbook CalculatorProject.xls. Turn this spreadsheet into a dynamic calculator which allows the user to vary the values (for A_0, r and N) in cells A2, A5, and A8 and outputs the value of an account accruing interest compounded annually to cell A11 by entering an appropriate formula.

3. In the workbook CalculatorProject.xls, consider the spreadsheet 'Present Value of Annuity.' Turn this spreadsheet into a calculator which allows the user to vary the values (for PMT, i, and n) in cells A2, A5, and A8 and outputs the present value of an annuity that pays the amount PV to cell A11 by entering an appropriate formula in that cell. Recall that the formula for the present value PV of an annuity that pays PMT per period for n periods at a periodic interest rate of i is given by

$$PV = PMT \frac{1-(1+i)^{-n}}{i}.$$

---

[1]Excel also has built-in functions for FV, PV, and PMT.

CHAPTER 5. THE MATHEMATICS OF FINANCE   94

> **You make the call:** Jenny would like to compare savings accounts at several area banks. However, the banks all compound differently. Your task is to make the spreadsheet 'Annual Yield' in `CalculatorProject.xls` into a dynamic 'annual yield calculator.' Then, use this calculator to fill in the remainder of the chart in Figure 5.3. Finally, decide with which bank Jenny should open an account.
>
> | Bank | Annual interest rate | Compounding method | Annual Yield |
> |---|---|---|---|
> | Alotolove | 7.25% | Quarterly | |
> | Bet-on-us | 6.25% | Daily | |
> | CashMax | 7.00% | Yearly | |
> | Deep Pockets | 6.75% | Monthly | |
>
> Figure 5.3: Computing annual yields at several area banks.
>
> *Hint:* You will want to look up (or derive) a formula for the annual yield of an account compounded k times a year at an annual interest rate of r.

5.2 Making Decisions Using Financial Spreadsheet Calculators

5.2.1 Offering a CD

[Download: AnnualYieldProject.xls]

Affluent Bank would like to offer a CD (certificate of deposit) with a daily compounding rate that has an annual yield of 6.5%. What annual nominal rate compounded daily should they use?

While it is possible to use some algebra to solve this problem, it may be even easier to use the `Goal Seek` tool in *Excel*. As Figure 5.4 shows, an annual rate of 6.5% compounded daily gives an annual yield (i.e. effective rate) of 6.72%. Hence, using the spreadsheet 'Annual Yield Calculator,' we need to seek an annual nominal rate lower than 6.5% to accomplish the task.

	A
1	Annual rate r
2	6.50%
3	
4	Compounding periods per year k
5	365
6	
7	Annual yield
8	6.72%

Figure 5.4: Using the annual yield calculator.

We begin by choosing `Goal Seek` under the `Tools` menu. Our goal will be to set cell `A8` to a value of 0.065 by changing cell `A2`. Upon doing this, we will find that an annual rate of 6.30% will do the trick.

1. If Affluent Bank would like to offer a CD with a monthly compounding rate that has an annual yield of 9%, what annual nominal rate compounded monthly should they use? Use `Goal Seek` in the spreadsheet calculator 'Annual Yield Calculator' to decide.

2. Affluent Bank would like to offer a CD with an annual nominal rate of 7.02% and an annual yield of 7.25%. Use `Solver`[2] in the spreadsheet 'Annual Yield Calculator' to compute how many times a year the money will need to be

---
[2]See chapter 3 for more information on `Solver`.

compounded. *Hints:* `Solver` will give you a decimal solution which you may wish to round. When using the `Solver` tool, you will want to set the target cell `A8` to a value of 0.0725 by changing cells `A5`. However, under `Options`, you will also need to set the tolerance to 0.01% in order to get close enough to the desired yield.

> **You make the call:** Affluent Bank would like to offer a CD with an annual nominal rate of 100% to its one millionth customer. They would also like this CD to have the maximum annual yield possible. Use the 'Annual Yield Calculator' and *Excel's* `Solver` tool to determine the maximum annual yield such a CD could produce. Does this yield have any relationship to the magical number 'e'? Should it? Explain.

5.2.2 Buying a House

[Download: BuyingHouseProject.xls]

Buying a house is a big financial decision one makes in life. Understanding a little about the financial aspects of buying a house surely cannot hurt.

Ann has her sights set on a $180,000 house on the outskirts of town. Before buying the house, it is useful (and almost always necessary) to have a down payment. In order to avoid paying PMI (private mortgage insurance), Ann would like to save 20% of the cost of the house, or $36,000, for a down payment. Of course, if Ann has $36,000 at the moment, this would not be a problem. But Ann, like most of us, does not have $36,000 and will have to start saving.

Ann does have $10,000 and can invest it in a savings account earning a hefty 8% annual interest compounded monthly. If Ann does not add any money to the account, how long will it take for her to have $36,000? Using the `Goal Seek` tool[3] in the spreadsheet 'Down Payment Method 1,' we see it would take Ann over 16 years before she could make such a purchase. This is not realistic as surely the real estate market will have changed drastically in that time and such a house would certainly cost more than $180,000.

Let us assume a more realistic scenario. We will assume that Ann has to save a certain amount per month to make a down payment and that the amount she needs to make as a down payment is changing due to changes in the real estate market.

Figure 5.5 illustrates a spreadsheet calculator that has been designed to help Ann decide how much she should save each month for three years at 4.8% annual interest in order to make a down payment of 20% on a house that is increasing in value 4% each year. Formulas occur in cells `A11`, `C8`, `C11`, and `C14`. Cell `A11` contains the Future Value formula

$$\text{=A2*((1+A5/12)^(A8*12)-1)/(A5/12)}$$

where the periodic interest rate is represented by `A5/12` and the number of periods is represented by `A8*12`. Cell `C8` contains the formula `=C2*(1+C5)^A8` which computes the value of the property after N (the value in cell `A8`) years. Cell `C14` simply contains the formula `=A11-C11`. This is the cell on which we `Goal Seek`. We set its value to 0 by changing the value in cell `A2`. The result, which appears in cell `A2` after the `Goal Seek`, is that Ann needs to save $1048.06 each month for three years in order to make a down payment of 20% on the house.

1. If Ann has $20,000, how long before she would have $36,000 assuming she can invest the money in an account bearing 8% annual interest compounded daily? Use the `Goal Seek` tool in the spreadsheet 'Down Payment Method 1' to decide.

---

[3]Set cell `A14` to a value of 36,000 by changing cell `A11`.

CHAPTER 5. THE MATHEMATICS OF FINANCE   98

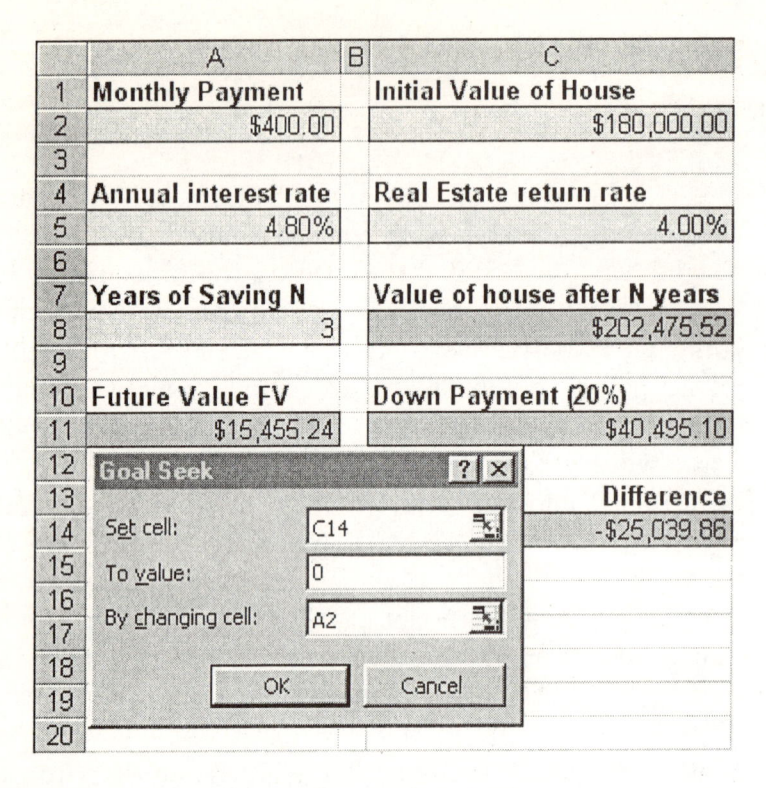

	A	B	C
1	Monthly Payment		Initial Value of House
2	$400.00		$180,000.00
3			
4	Annual interest rate		Real Estate return rate
5	4.80%		4.00%
6			
7	Years of Saving N		Value of house after N years
8	3		$202,475.52
9			
10	Future Value FV		Down Payment (20%)
11	$15,455.24		$40,495.10
12			
13			Difference
14			-$25,039.86

Goal Seek dialog:
- Set cell: C14
- To value: 0
- By changing cell: A2

Figure 5.5: Deciding monthly payments in saving for the down payment on a house.

2. If real estate in Ann's town is increasing in value at a rate of 6% per year and Ann is only able to save at an interest rate of 4.8% for 2 years before making a 20% down payment on a house currently valued at $150,000, how much will Ann need to save each month? Use the `Goal Seek` tool in the spreadsheet 'Down Payment Method 2' to decide.

3. Suppose that Ann knows that she can only save $800 per month on a down payment for a house currently valued at $150,000 that is increasing in value at a rate of 5% per year. She can get an annual interest rate of 6.5% on her savings from her local bank. How many years will pass before Ann can make a down payment on such a house? Use `Goal Seek` to decide.

> **You make the call:** Suppose that real estate prices in Ann's town are currently *decreasing* at a rate of 5% per year and Ann can save at an interest rate of 3% for two years before making a 5% down payment on a house currently valued at $200,000. Modify the spreadsheet 'Down Payment Method 2' and use `Goal Seek` to decide how much Ann needs to save each month. What if Ann would like to buy in one year's time?

CHAPTER 5. THE MATHEMATICS OF FINANCE

5.2.3 Winning the Lottery

[Download: LotteryProject.xls]

People in several states play the Powerball lottery. In Powerball, the chances of winning are quite slim (we will visit the question of exactly how slim later), but *if* you win, you win a large sum of money. A typical jackpot might consist of a $55 million dollar prize. A single winner of this prize must choose between a 25-year annuity with a present value of $55 million dollars or a $30 million dollar cash prize.[4]

Imagine for a moment that you have won a typical Powerball jackpot. Would you want to choose the cash prize or the annuity? Although tax considerations may play into your decision, we will assume they do not. The main factor in your decision then, we assume, is the rate of return you believe you could achieve with the cash option. Could the $30,000,000 earn 5% interest? 6%? How safely do you want to invest this money?

	A	B	C
1	Annuity Prize		Yearly Payment
2	$55,000,000.00		$2,200,000.00
3			
4			Yearly interest rate
5			5.3322%
6			
7			Number of years of annuity
8			25
9			
10			Present Value of all payments
11			$30,000,000.00

Figure 5.6: Deciding how to collect winnings from Powerball.

The spreadsheet calculator shown in Figure 5.6 can help an individual decide which option is right for them. Using the `Goal Seek` tool, we set cell `C11` to a value of $30,000,000 by changing the interest rate in cell `C5`. The formula in cell `C11` which allows us to do this is a present value formula

$$\mathtt{=C2*(1-(1+C5)\wedge(-C8))/C5}$$

where the value in cell `C2` is the yearly payment, the value in cell `C5` represents the annual interest rate, and the value in `C8` represents the number of years which the annuity covers. Another key formula in this spreadsheet occurs in cell `C2`. This

---

[4]Source: www.powerball.com (5/24/01)

formula, `A2/C8`, computes the size of the equal yearly payments that are made for an annuity prize the size of $55,000,000.

As Figure 5.6 indicates, a winner of this Powerball lottery should choose the cash option if they think they could invest it safely with an annual yield better than 5.33%.

1. In January of 2001, Linda Calliea of Michigan won *The Big Game* lottery jackpot. The prize was her choice of a $107,000,000 26-year annuity or a $57,775,399 cash option. Use the `Goal Seek` tool and the spreadsheet 'Powerball' to determine the annual yield for this annuity.

2. On May 18, 2001, Nicholas C. Traina won the New Jersey Pick 6 Lotto jackpot. His prize options were $892,312 in cash or a 30-year $2,000,000 annuity. Use the `Goal Seek` tool and the spreadsheet 'Powerball' to determine the annual yield for this annuity.

3. The New Hampshire Lottery has a game it calls 'Cash 4 Life' in which it offers a winner $1,000 a week for life. The spreadsheet 'Cash 4 Life' helps calculate the true value of such an event. In the spreadsheet, cell `C11` contains the formula

    `=C2*(1-(1+C5/52)^(-C8*52))/(C5/52)`.

Explain where this formula comes from. Then, estimate how many years remain in your life and use the spreadsheet to compute the present cash value of such a prize if you were to win.

> **You make the call:** A new lottery game has appeared in your home state. The grand prize is an annuity of $10,000 a month for life. The cash option is $3,000,000. Fill in the last formula of the spreadsheet 'Monthly Cash' and then use `Goal Seek` to estimate the annual yield of the annuity. Which payment option would you choose? Answers will obviously vary!

CHAPTER 5. THE MATHEMATICS OF FINANCE 101

5.3 Amortization Schedules

[Download: AmortizationProject.xls]

Many times in life, consumers decide to finance debt by making regular payments of fixed size. Such a process is called **amortization**. The design of amortization tables with a spreadsheet beautifully illustrates the power of modern technology.

As a simple example, we consider the construction of an amortization table for a $5,000 loan at 9% annual interest to be paid off with 12 equal monthly payments as illustrated in Figure 5.7 and the spreadsheet 'Amortization.'

	A	B	C	D	E	F	G	H
1	Loan Amount	$5,000.00		Annual Interest Rate	9.00%		Years	1
2								
3	Payment	$437.26		Number of Payments	12			
4								
5	Payment Number	Payment	Interest	Balance Reduction	Unpaid Balance		Total Interest	
6	0	$0.00	$0.00	$0.00	$5,000.00		$0.00	
7	1	$437.26	$37.50	$399.76	$4,600.24		$37.50	
8	2	$437.26	$34.50	$402.76	$4,197.49		$72.00	
9	3	$437.26	$31.48	$405.78	$3,791.71		$103.48	
10	4	$437.26	$28.44	$408.82	$3,382.89		$131.92	
11	5	$437.26	$25.37	$411.89	$2,971.01		$157.29	
12	6	$437.26	$22.28	$414.97	$2,556.03		$179.58	
13	7	$437.26	$19.17	$418.09	$2,137.94		$198.75	
14	8	$437.26	$16.03	$421.22	$1,716.72		$214.78	
15	9	$437.26	$12.88	$424.38	$1,292.34		$227.66	
16	10	$437.26	$9.69	$427.56	$864.77		$237.35	
17	11	$437.26	$6.49	$430.77	$434.00		$243.83	
18	12	$437.26	$3.26	$434.00	$0.00		$247.09	

Figure 5.7: Amortization table for a $5,000 debt paid off at 9% annual interest over 12 months.

The first task in creating such a table is to decide what the equal monthly payments must be. Such a loan is, of course, an ordinary annuity with a present value of $5,000. Hence, the payment is given by

$$PMT = PV \frac{i}{1-(1+i)^{-n}} = 5000 \frac{0.09/12}{1-(1+0.09/12)^{-12}}.$$

We calculate this in cell B3 of the spreadsheet using the formula

`=B1*((E1/12)/(1-(1+E1/12)^(-H1*12)))`

or using the built-in PMT function

$$\text{=PMT(E1/12, 12*H1, B1, 0)}.$$

The number of payments to be made on the loan is obviously given by 12 times the number of years the loan is over.

	A	B	C	D	E	F	G
5	Payment Number	Payment	Interest	Balance Reduction	Unpaid		Total Interest
6	0	0	0	0	=B1		0
7	=A6+1	=$B$3	=E6*$E$1/12	=B7-C7	=E6-D7		=SUM($C$6:C7)

Figure 5.8: Constructing the first two lines of an amortization table in *Excel*.

We continue construction of the amortization table by entering the formulas in the appropriate cells as shown in Figure 5.8. The real key to these formulas is knowing when to use absolute references and when to use the relative references. For example, in cell C7 when computing the interest accumulated during the first month we use the formula =E6*$E$1/12 because this will later be copied down column C. In the computation of the interest, the interest rate (in cell E1) remains fixed; however, the amount subject to interest decreases as we pay off the debt. Hence, we use the relative reference E6 to refer to the unpaid balance. As another example, notice that in the unpaid balance column E, we use the relative references =E6-D7 since this amount is calculated by the previous unpaid balance minus the current balance reduction.

The final, and most powerful, step in the construction of such a table is to highlight the cells A7 through G7 and copy them down until the number of payments meets the required number to pay off the loan (12 times the number of years of the loan).

The first time a spreadsheet user successfully attempts this copying process is life-changing experience. Imagine how long it would take to produce such a table with a simple calculator or with just pencil and paper! One will understand why it is that people call a spreadsheet a "killer application" for the personal computer. This very experience is what drove the development of the personal computer and made Bill Gates a wealthy man.

1. Alter the spreadsheet 'Amortization' to produce a monthly amortization table for a 4-year $15,500 car loan financed at 9.3% annual interest. Suppose that interest on this loan could be tax deducted. How much interest is paid on this loan during the first year? How about during the second year?

2. Alter the spreadsheet 'Amortization' to produce a monthly amortization table for a 30-year $125,000 home loan financed at 7.1% annual interest. How much interest is paid over the life of the loan?

CHAPTER 5. THE MATHEMATICS OF FINANCE 103

3. Assuming that interest on a 30-year $125,000 home loan financed at 7.1% annual interest can be deducted, use the spreadsheet generated above to compute how much interest is paid during the 4th year of the loan.

4. Use the spreadsheet 'Amortization' to produce a chart similar to that shown in Figure 5.9 showing the unpaid balance over the course of the 360 payments made in a 30-year, $125,000 home loan financed at 7.1% annual interest. Does the shape of the graph surprise you? What shape did you expect?

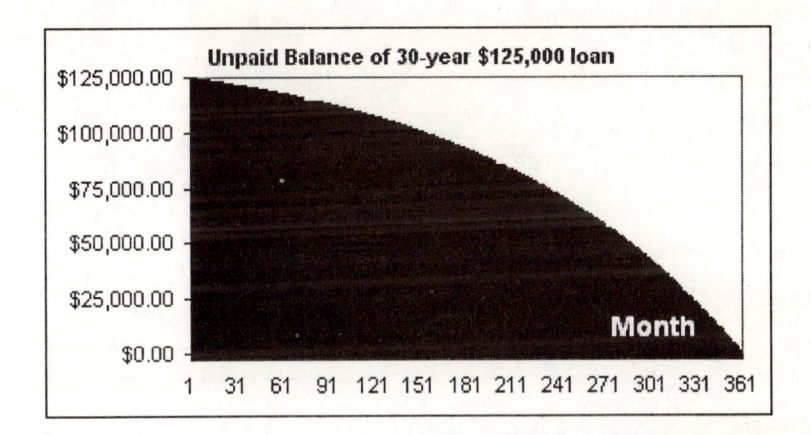

Figure 5.9: Charting the unpaid balance of a 30-year $125,000 home loan.

You make the call: Using the spreadsheet 'Home Loan' containing the chart as shown in Figure 5.9, decide how the shape of the chart changes if the annual interest rate is doubled to 14.2%. What if the annual interest rate is halved to 3.55%? What happens to the shape of this graph as the interest rate gets smaller and smaller? What happens to the shape of the graph as the interest rate gets larger and larger? Which of these shapes do you think the average home owner believes represents the unpaid balance of their home loan?

5.4 IRA's

[Download: IRAProject.xls]

In planning for retirement, one decision nearly everyone needs to make is whether to start an IRA (Individual Retirement Account) or not. Because of tax advantages, many people decide to start an IRA at some point of their life.

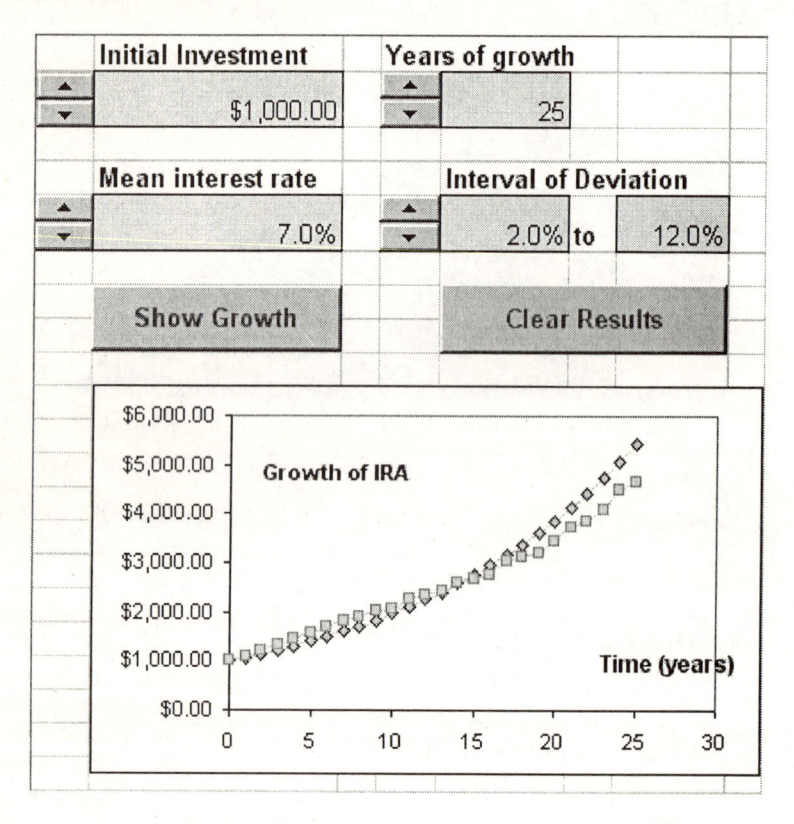

Figure 5.10: Modeling growth of $1,000 in an IRA.

One model for the growth of a $1,000 IRA deposit over 25 years is to assume that it will earn a constant rate r of return. In such a model, we have an explicit formula for the amount of money in the IRA after t years ($0 \leq t \leq 25$). If the account has the interest compounded yearly, then

$$A(t) = 1000 \left(1 + r\right)^t$$

represents the amount in the account after t years.

Another, perhaps better, model of the growth of a $1,000 IRA deposit over 25 years

CHAPTER 5. THE MATHEMATICS OF FINANCE   105

is to assume that it will annually return rate r randomly, but uniformly,[5] distributed between $-d + r_0$ and $r_0 + d$ for some constant rate r_0 and fixed deviation d. For example, we could assume that each year the IRA has a rate of return between 2% and 12%. In that case, $r_0 = 7\%$ and $d = 5\%$. Using the random number generator in *Excel* allows us to simulate the growth of the $1,000 over the 25 years. A spreadsheet 'Growth of an IRA' which does this is shown in Figure 5.10. Notice how the simulated growth is similar to the growth one would see using a fixed interest rate of 7%. In some years, the IRA returns better than 7%, in some years, the return is worse.

1. Use the spreadsheet 'Growth of an IRA' to simulate the growth of a single $2,000 IRA deposit growing for 40 years at an interest rate uniformly varying between 4% and 6%. How does growth in such an account compare to an account having an interest rate uniformly varying between -5% and 15%?

2. Simulate the growth of a single $2,000 IRA deposit growing for 40 years at an interest rate varying uniformly between -15% and 25%. Draw a diagram which graphically illustrates how the graph of this simulated growth is related to the graphs of the functions $A_1(t) = 2000(0.085)^t$ and $A_2(t) = 2000(1.25)^t$.

3. The very first decision one is confronted with after they have decided to start an IRA is whether it should be a Roth IRA[6] or a traditional IRA. Sometimes, the decision is a complicated one and is usually best left to a tax accountant.

   While there are several technical differences between Roth IRA's and traditional IRA's, the main difference is in taxation. In a traditional (deductible) IRA, a deposit using pre-tax earnings is made and grows tax free until withdrawl at which time the entire IRA is taxed as income. In a Roth IRA, a deposit is made using after-tax earnings and grows tax free until it is withdrawn. There is no tax on the withdrawl.[7]

   To illustrate the difference, assume that Shelly is planning on making a once in a lifetime deposit in an IRA. She has $2,000 burning a hole in her pocket and would like to build a nest egg for retirement with it. Shelly is in the 28% tax bracket. Following the advice of her friends, she invests the $2,000 in a Roth IRA. Actually, she pays the federal government (.28)($2,000)=$560 in taxes and puts the remaining $1,440 in an interest bearing bank account.

   Sammy, who is the same age and in the same tax bracket as Shelly, is planning on making a once-in-a-lifetime $2,000 deposit in a traditional IRA in the same bank on the same day. He is planning on retiring at the same time as Shelly.

---

[5] Other distributions could also be assumed.
[6] Rother IRA's, which came to exist in 1998, are named after their sponsor, Senator William Roth of Delaware.
[7] Conditions may vary. This is the basic idea.

CHAPTER 5. THE MATHEMATICS OF FINANCE 106

Assume that both Sammy and Shelly will remain in the same tax bracket (28%) when they retire.

Use the spreadsheet 'Roth vs. Traditional' in the workbook `IRAProject.xls` to decide who made the better decision. Does it matter how much each have to initially invest? Is the tax bracket relevant? How about the interest rate?

Based on the information you have, what factor(s) might influence your Roth vs. Traditional IRA decision?

You make the call: As a financial planner, you have advised a young client to put her IRA in a stock index fund which has historically returned 7% per year, but whose yearly return can have a large deviation. After 7 years of watching her fund perform, the client shows you the chart in Figure 5.11 comparing her actual return to what you had 'promised' her 7 years ago. How might you try to convince your client that she should retain your services? Can you use the spreadsheet 'Growth of an IRA' to help?

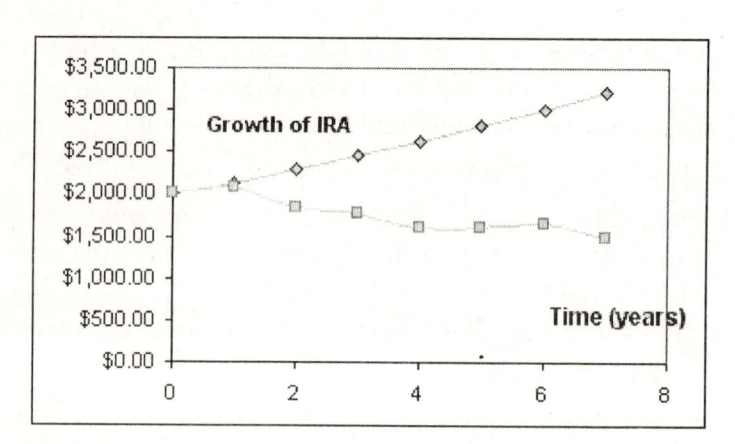

Figure 5.11: Growth of a client's IRA after 7 years.

Chapter 6

Probability Distributions

6.1 The Binomial Distribution

[Download: BinomialProject.xls]

In many situations related to probability there are exactly two possible outcomes. When a coin is tossed, it comes up heads or tails. An HIV test comes back positive or negative. In the game of basketball, a free throw is either made or not made.

A **binomial experiment** is a probability experiment in which each of n trials has two possible outcomes. There is a probability p of success and a probability $1 - p$ of failure. Further, in a binomial experiment we require that the n trials are independent of each other. A **binomial distribution** describes the results of a binomial experiment.

In a binomial experiment, the probability of having x successes in n independent trials where the probability of success on any given trial is p is given by

$$P(x) = {_nC_x} \cdot p^x \cdot (1-p)^{n-x}.$$

We often use $q = 1 - p$ to denote the probability of failure.

Consider a simple experiment consisting of having Los Angeles Laker basketball player Shaquille O'Neal shoot 10 free throws.[1] During the 2000-2001 season, Shaq made approximately 51% of his free throws.[2] If we were to repeat this experiment, we would expect that Shaq making 5 of the 10 free throws would be the most common result. We would not expect Shaq to make 9 or 10 of the 10 free throws very often in performing this experiment.

Figure 6.1 shows how we can use a spreadsheet to better understand this free throw shooting experiment. The key formula occurs in cell `A4`:

---

[1] We will assume these free throws are independent and that Shaq does not get into a 'groove.'
[2] Source: www.nba.com

CHAPTER 6. PROBABILITY DISTRIBUTIONS

=BINOMDIST(A4,$I$1,$C$1,FALSE)

Excel has the Binomial distribution built in and we can access the values by using the BINOMDIST function. This particular formula returns the probability of having exactly 0 (the value in A4) successes in 10 attempts where the probability of success on any given attempt is 0.51 (the value in $C$1).

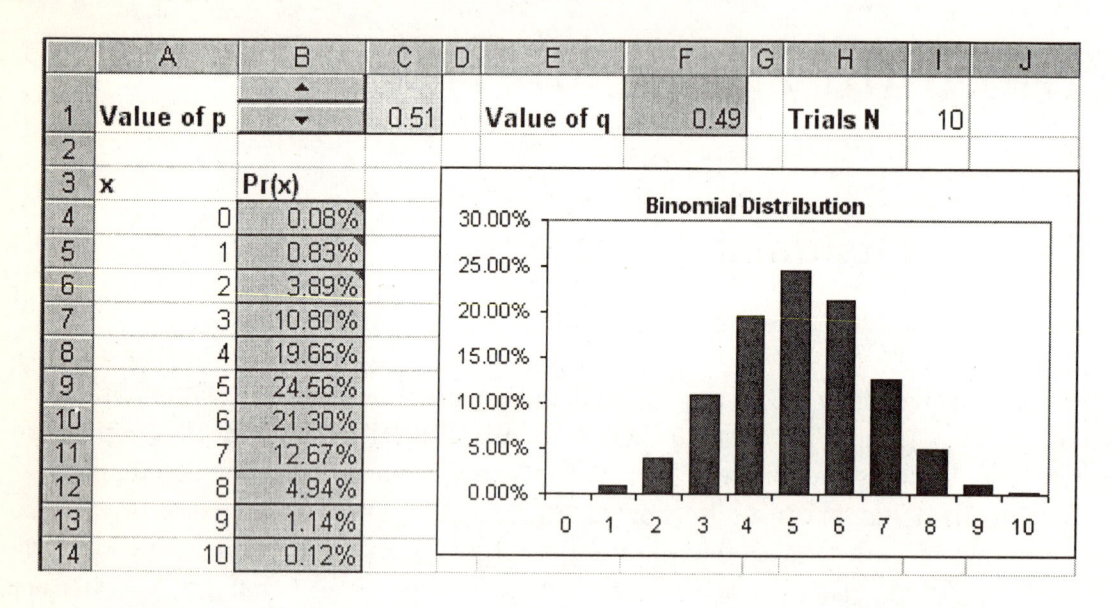

	A	B	C	D	E	F	G	H	I	J
1	Value of p		0.51		Value of q	0.49		Trials N	10	
2										
3	x	Pr(x)								
4	0	0.08%								
5	1	0.83%								
6	2	3.89%								
7	3	10.80%								
8	4	19.66%								
9	5	24.56%								
10	6	21.30%								
11	7	12.67%								
12	8	4.94%								
13	9	1.14%								
14	10	0.12%								

Figure 6.1: Probable results of having Shaq shoot 10 free throws.

The spreadsheet 'Simulation' within the workbook BinomialProject.xls shows how a large number of binomial trials results in a distribution similar to the binomial distribution. For example, if we were to have Shaq shoot 10 free throws 50 times (for a total of 500 free throws), the results can be seen together with the binomial distribution in Figure 6.2. In the actual spreadsheet, note how the experimental values can change, but the binomial distribution does not. This is the difference between theory and reality.

On average, how many free throws should we expect Shaq to make in 10 attempts? To compute this expected value in *Excel*, we use the SUMPRODUCT command in cells B16 and C16 of the spreadsheet 'Simulation.' Note how the formula =SUMPRODUCT(A4:A14,C4:C14) in cell C16 computes the average number of free throws made per 10 attempts in the simulation.

1. During the 2000-2001 NBA season, Toronto Raptor basketball player Vince Carter made approximately 76% of his free throws. If we conducted an experiment in which he shot exactly 10 free throws, alter the spreadsheet 'Shaq' to

CHAPTER 6. PROBABILITY DISTRIBUTIONS

determine the probability of Vince making exactly 8 of them. What would his chances be of making 2 or fewer free throws?

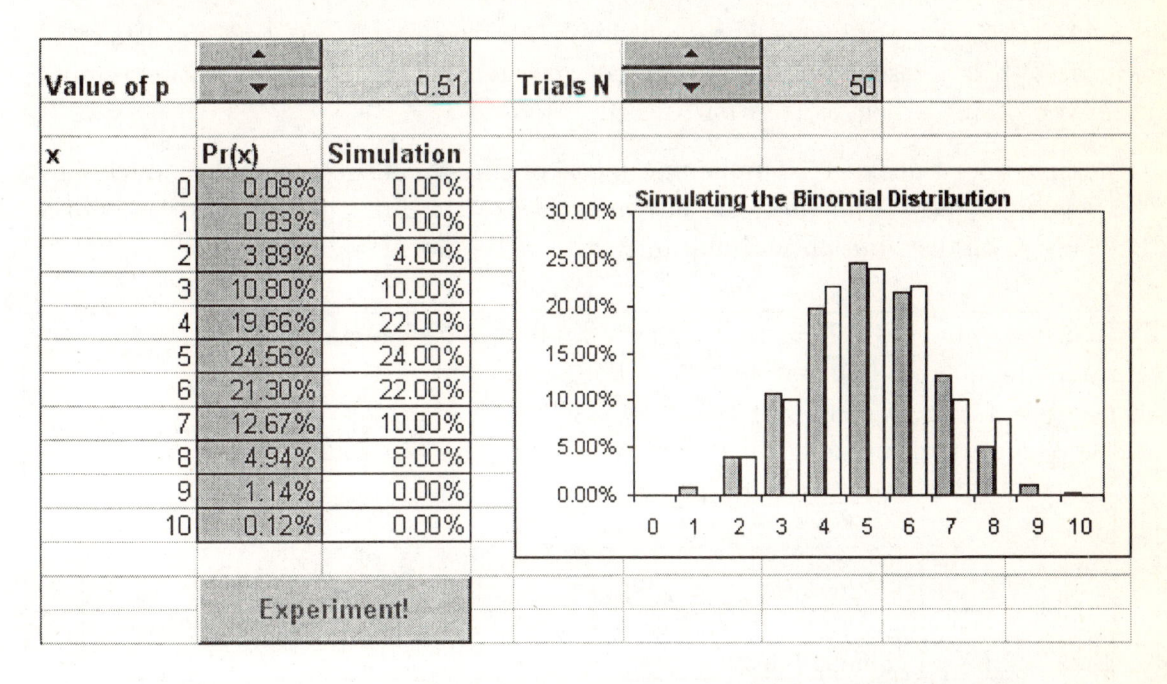

Value of p		0.51	Trials N		50
x	Pr(x)	Simulation			
0	0.08%	0.00%			
1	0.83%	0.00%			
2	3.89%	4.00%			
3	10.80%	10.00%			
4	19.66%	22.00%			
5	24.56%	24.00%			
6	21.30%	22.00%			
7	12.67%	10.00%			
8	4.94%	8.00%			
9	1.14%	0.00%			
10	0.12%	0.00%			
	Experiment!				

Figure 6.2: Shaq experiments at shooting 10 free throws 50 times.

2. Imagine a stadium full of people each flipping a fair coin 10 times. Using the spreadsheet 'Shaq,' decide what percentage of these people we should expect to have heads landing exactly 7 times? 9 times or more?

3. In the year 2000, it was estimated that approximately 12% of the urban population in Haiti was living with HIV/AIDS.[3] Alter the spreadsheet 'Shaq' to determine the likelyhood that in a random sample of 10 urban Haitians, at least one person would have HIV/AIDS.

4. Use the spreadsheet 'Shaq' to determine how the binomial distribution having $n = 10$ and $p = 0.4$ is related to the binomial distribution having $n = 10$ and $p = 0.6$. How about if $p = 0.35$ and $p = 0.65$? If $p = 0.3$ and $p = 0.7$? Can you draw any conclusions?

5. Suppose Vince Carter, a.k.a. 76% free throw shooter, were to shoot one set of 10 free throws. Use the spreadsheet 'Simulate' to simulate how many he would make. What is the actual probability of him making that many? If you were

---
[3]Source: Population Reference Bureau

CHAPTER 6. PROBABILITY DISTRIBUTIONS 110

to run the experiment a few times using the spreadsheet, does he ever make 10 free throws? Would he ever make 0? Explain.

6. Describe what happens when you simulate Vince Carter shooting 450 sets of 10 free throws (assuming his arms do not get tired!). Does this distribution remind you of any other distribution?

7. How does the expected value in cell B16 of the spreadsheet 'Simulation' change as p changes? Can you form any hypothesis regarding the expected value of a binomial distribution with parameters $n = 10$ and p?

You make the call: In an attempt to study the 12% of the urban Haitian population living with HIV/AIDS, you send 5 teams across Haiti who are all instructed to randomly select 10 Haitians. Four of the five teams find that nobody in their sample has HIV/AIDS as shown in the simulation illustrated in Figure 6.3.

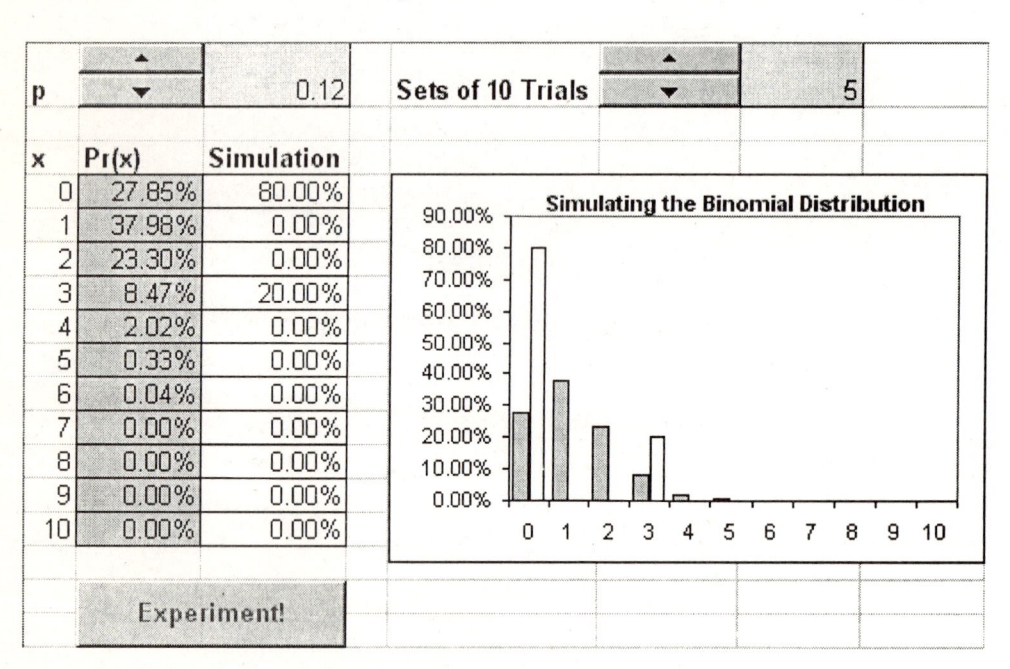

Figure 6.3: Studying HIV/AIDS in urban Haiti.

How many of the teams did you expect to have fail at finding at least one person having HIV/AIDS? Use the spreadsheet 'Simulate' to send out another 5 teams. What happened this time? Explain these results to your boss.

6.2 The Negative Binomial Distribution

[Download: NegativeBinomialProject.xls]

Consider a simple experiment consisting of having Los Angeles Laker basketball player Shaquille O'Neal shoot free throws.[4] How long might we have to wait before Shaq was able to make 3 free throws? What is the probability that we would have to wait 7 shots? The negative binomial distribution can be used to answer questions such as these.

During the 2000-2001 season, Shaq made approximately $p = 51\%$ of his free throws.[5] Let's begin by considering the problem of finding the probability that it would take four free throws before Shaq could make two. There are 3 possible ways this can happen. We denote them using 'S' for success and 'F' for failure.

$$SFFS$$
$$FSFS$$
$$FFSS$$

Clearly there is a pattern here. In fact, the number 3 comes from the fact that there are 3 ways to make any one of the first 3 shots. So, the probability of Shaq would take 4 free throws before making 2 of them is

$$3p^2(1-p)^2.$$

The probability that Shaq would take 7 free throws before making 3 of them is

$$_6C_2 \cdot p^3 \cdot (1-p)^4$$

where the $_6C_2$ comes from the fact that we are counting the number of ways that Shaq can make 2 of his first 6 shots (in any order).

In general, the probability that it will take t trials before we have r successes ($t \geq r$) is given by

$$_{r-1}C_{t-1} \cdot p^r \cdot (1-p)^{t-r}.$$

For a given number r, we can better understand this distribution graphically with the aid of *Excel*. The key formula, which is copied down column B of the spreadsheet 'Shaq' in the workbook `NegativeBinomialProject.xls` occurs in cell B4. The formula

```
=NEGBINOMDIST(A4-$F$1,$F$1,$C$1)
```

---

[4]We will assume these free throws are independent events and that Shaq does not get into a 'groove.'

[5]Source: www.nba.com

CHAPTER 6. PROBABILITY DISTRIBUTIONS 112

uses the negative binomial function which returns the probability that it will take t trials before we have r successes. The first parameter of this function refers to the number of 'failures' $t - r$, the second parameter represents the number of successes r, and the last parameter represents p. Figure 6.4 shows the negative binomial distribution for $p = 0.51$ and $r = 3$. From Figure 6.4, we see that there is a 10.86% chance that Shaq would not make his third free throw until exactly his seventh attempt and that there is an 86.73% chance that it will take more than three free throws until Shaq makes three.

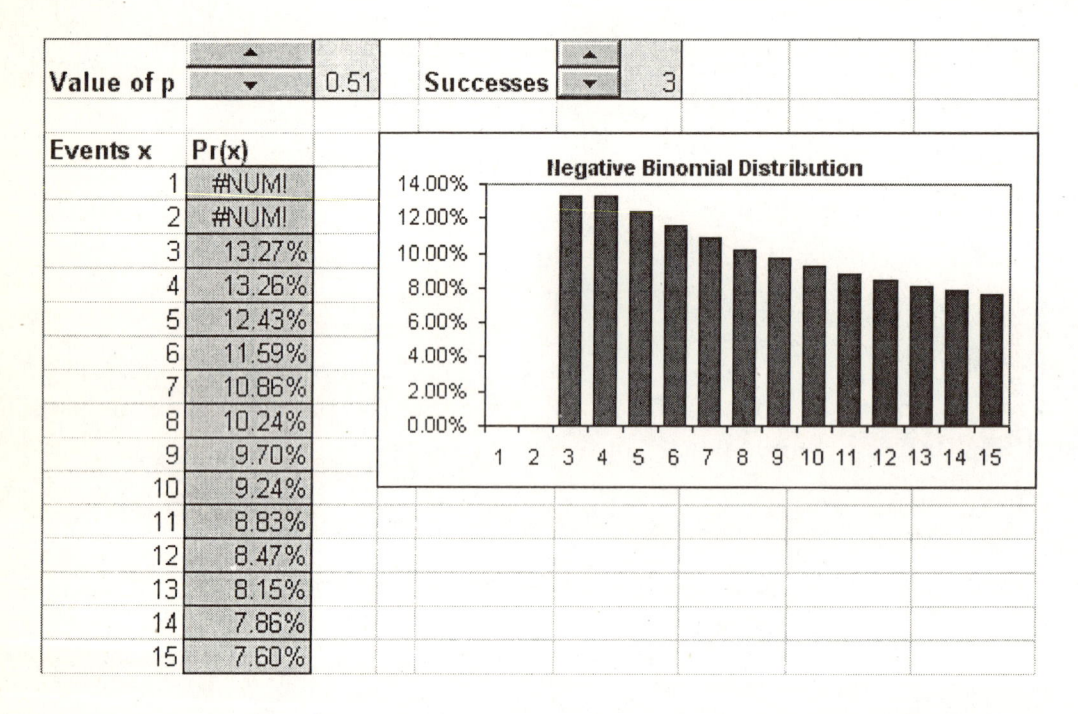

Value of p	0.51	Successes	3

Events x	Pr(x)
1	#NUM!
2	#NUM!
3	13.27%
4	13.26%
5	12.43%
6	11.59%
7	10.86%
8	10.24%
9	9.70%
10	9.24%
11	8.83%
12	8.47%
13	8.15%
14	7.86%
15	7.60%

Figure 6.4: How long it would probably take for Shaq to make 3 free throws.

The spreadsheet 'Simulation' shows how a large number of experiments can lead to a distribution similar to the negative binomial distribution. For example, if we were to repeat 100 times the experiment of having Shaq shoot until he make 3 free throws, we might get the results similar to the negative binomial distribution as shown in Figure 6.5.

1. During the 2000-2001 NBA season, Toronto Raptor basketball player Vince Carter made approximately 76% of his free throws. Alter the spreadsheet 'Shaq' in the workbook `NegativeBinomialProject.xls` to determine the probability that it would take Vince seven free throw attempts in order to make three. How likely is he to make his first three attempts?

CHAPTER 6. PROBABILITY DISTRIBUTIONS

2. Shooting free throws at a rate of about 93%, Reggie Miller of the Indiana Pacers led the NBA in free throw percentage during the 2000-2001 NBA season. Use the spreadsheet 'Shaq' to determine the probability that it would take Reggie seven free throw attempts in order to make three. How likely is it to take Reggie 15 shots before making 3 free throws?

3. As a general rule, for a fixed value of r (say $r = 3$), how does the negative binomial distribution change as the value of p increases? Use the spreadsheet 'Shaq' to help you form your hypothesis.

4. As a general rule, for a fixed value of p (say $p = 0.51$), how does the negative binomial distribution change as the value of r increases?

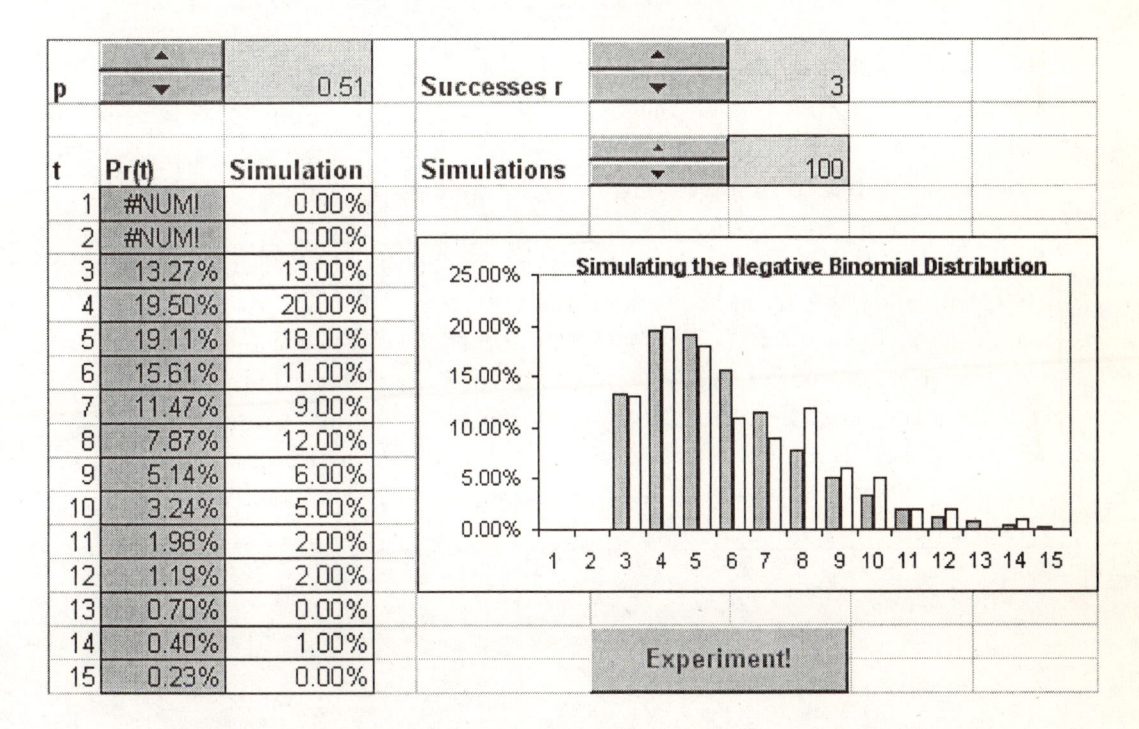

p		0.51	Successes r		3
t	Pr(t)	Simulation	Simulations		100
1	#NUM!	0.00%			
2	#NUM!	0.00%			
3	13.27%	13.00%			
4	19.50%	20.00%			
5	19.11%	18.00%			
6	15.61%	11.00%			
7	11.47%	9.00%			
8	7.87%	12.00%			
9	5.14%	6.00%			
10	3.24%	5.00%			
11	1.98%	2.00%			
12	1.19%	2.00%			
13	0.70%	0.00%			
14	0.40%	1.00%			
15	0.23%	0.00%			

Figure 6.5: Having Shaq perform an experiment 100 times.

5. According to the simulation from Figure 6.5, how many times out of the 100 trial experiments did Shaq not make his third free throw until his tenth attempt? How many times should we expect to wait until exactly his tenth attempt to make his third free throw?

6. Run a simulation in which we experiment 50 times with Reggie Miller, a.k.a. 93% free throw shooter, attempting to make 10 free throws. In how many of

CHAPTER 6. PROBABILITY DISTRIBUTIONS

the 50 experiments does he make his first 10 in a row? In how many of these 50 experiments should we expect that he make 50 in a row?

7. If Shaq, a.k.a. 51% free throw shooter, were to attempt 80 free throws, we might ask how many free throws that we would be 95% certain he could make (meaning if he shoots 80 free throws 100 times, in theory he would make at least this number 95 out of the 100 times). 10? Certainly more than that? 70? Not so fast! 40? Thankfully, there is an *Excel* function `CRITBINOM` that can compute this for us. In order to compute how many free throws we would be 95% certain Shaq could make, we compute

$$=\texttt{CRITBINOM(80,0.51,0.95)}.$$

Finish developing the dynamic spreadsheet 'With Certainty' so that it will compute how many of 80 free throws we would be 95% confident of Shaq making. How many of the 80 would we be as sure that Vince Carter would make? How is this idea related to quality control in the making of widgets?

> **You make the call:** Midway through the 2000-2001 NBA season, Shaq was shooting free throws at a rate of 41%. One day after hiring a new shooting coach, he set a record for the worst ever free throw shooting performance in NBA history (dethroning Wilt Chamberlain) at 0 for 11 against Seattle. Alter the spreadsheet 'Shaq' to determine the probability that it would take Shaq 12 free throw attempts in order to make just one. Do you think something other than probability was at work here?

CHAPTER 6. PROBABILITY DISTRIBUTIONS 115

6.3 SuperLoserLotto

[Download: SuperLoserLottoProject.xls]

Like many jackpot lotteries, Texas's CASH 5 lottery game is easy to understand and play. In fact, they claim

> *You can win exciting CASH prizes just by matching 3, 4, or 5 numbers from a field of 39.*

A spreadsheet can help us decide just how easy this is to do. It can also help us compare how the odds in Texas compare to that of other state lotteries. The basic probability computation is much the same everywhere. The object is to match x balls by choosing n where M balls are chosen randomly **without replacement** from an urn containing N balls. For example, to win \$25[6] in the Texas CASH 5 game, we need to choose $n = 5$ balls and match $x = 3$ of the $M = 5$ balls chosen from an urn containing $N = 39$ balls (in any order). The probability of matching exactly 3 of the 5 balls drawn from the urn is

$$\frac{(\text{number of ways of getting 3 successes})(\text{number of ways of getting 2 failures})}{\text{number of ways of selecting 5 balls from 39}}.$$

Using combinations, the probability of success is easy to write as

$$\frac{(_5C_3) \cdot (_{36}C_2)}{_{39}C_5} \approx 0.009743694$$

or about 1 in 103. In general, the chances of success[7] are

$$\frac{(_MC_x) \cdot (_{N-M}C_{n-x})}{_NC_n}.$$

Figure 6.6 illustrates how we can let a spreadsheet compute these probabilities for us. The key formulas are in cells A4 and B4. In cell A4, we've entered

=COMBIN($B$2,$C$2)*COMBIN($A$2-$B$2,$B$2-$C$2)/COMBIN($A$2,$B$2)

where the *Excel* syntax COMBIN(n,r) is the equivalent of the mathematical notation $_nC_r$ for a combination.[8] In cell B4, we have used the =ROUNDUP(1/$A$2,1) command to round the odds up to the next nearest tenth (regardless of the size of the remaining decimal part).

---

[6]Average prize.
[7]see section 6.4.
[8]In section 6.4, we use *Excel*'s HYPGEODIST function.

CHAPTER 6. PROBABILITY DISTRIBUTIONS   116

	A	B	C
1	Balls in Urn	Number of balls drawn	Number of balls to be matched
2	39	5	3
3	Probability	Odds (1 in ...)	
4	0.00974369	102.7	
5			
6	# Matched	Probability of matching	Odds (1 in ...)
7	0	0.48328722	2.1
8	1	0.40273935	2.5
9	2	0.103932736	9.7
10	3	0.009743694	102.7
11	4	0.000295263	3386.9
12	5	1.73684E-06	575757

Figure 6.6: What are the chances of winning the Texas CASH 5 game?

Now, imagine that you would like to educate the public about the probability of winning lottery games such as the Texas CASH 5. A table such as that shown in Figure 6.6 can help, but a chart such as that shown in Figure 6.7 can speak volumes.

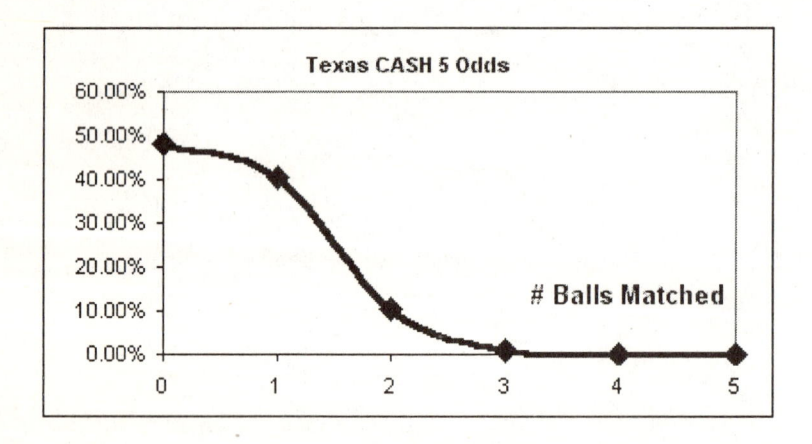

Figure 6.7: Charting the chances of winning the Texas CASH 5 game.

The table in Figure 6.6 is generated by using the same formula in cell B7 as was used in cell A4. The only difference is that instead of referring to the absolute cell $C$2, we refer to the relative cell A7. Copying this formula down column B produces the required results. Of course, a simple check shows that the sum of the values in column B is 1.

Drawing the chart in Figure 6.7 can be done by highlighting cells A7 through B12. More help on plotting such data can be found in the appendix to chapter 1.

CHAPTER 6. PROBABILITY DISTRIBUTIONS

1. Use the spreadsheet 'Lottery Odds' to answer the following questions regarding state lotteries.

   (a) What is the probability of matching 4 of 5 balls drawn in the Texas CASH 5 game?

   (b) In California, Fantasy 5 is a game where you match 5 numbers chosen without replacement out of a field of 39. What is the probability of winning such a game?

   (c) In Iowa's $100,000 Cash game, you try to match 2,3,4, or 5 numbers to 5 numbers chosen without replacement from a field of 35. The Iowa Lottery website gives the following table regarding odds of winning each prize.

Match	Win	Odds
5	$100,000	1 in 324,632
4	$100	1 in 2,164
3	$5	1 in 74
2	Free Play	1 in 8

   Is the Iowa Lottery website is correct or have they 'stretched the truth' a bit? Explain.

   (d) In Florida's Lotto, you try to match 3,4,5 or 6 numbers to 6 numbers chosen without replacement from a field of 53. Use the spreadsheet 'Lottery Odds' to fill in the following table regarding odds of winning each prize.

Match	Win	Odds
6	Jackpot	
5	$5,000	
4	$70	
3	$5	

   Do you have a better chance of winning exactly $5 in Iowa's $100,000 cash game or in Florida's Lotto? Why do you suspect this is the case?

2. Use *Excel* to draw a chart similar to Figure 6.7 for the Florida Lotto in which you try to match 3,4,5 or 6 numbers to 6 numbers chosen without replacement from a field of 53.

> **You make the call:** In the Texas CASH 5 game, the probability of matching 3,4, or 5 balls is about 1/100. We would like to design a new lottery game called SuperLoserLotto, in which the object is to match 0,1, or 2 balls to those drawn without replacment from an urn containing 50 balls. Use the spreadsheet 'SuperLoserLotto' in order to decide how many balls x should be drawn so that the probability of matching 0,1, or 2 balls is less than 1/100. In such a game, what are the odds of matching 0 balls to the x balls drawn?

6.4 The Hypergeometric Distribution

[Download: HypergeometricProject.xls]

In the case of binomial distribution, we have assumed that p, the probability of 'success' remains constant from one trial to the next. In other words, we carried out sampling **with replacement**.

An example of sampling **with replacement** would be the Minnesota lottery's Daily 3 game. The objective of this game is to match 3 digits (0-9) which are drawn randomly from a bin with replacement. A winning combination might be 303 (where the order the digits are drawn matters). The probability of winning the Daily 3 game is $(0.1)^{10} = 0.001$. The probability of matching 0,1,2, or 3 numbers is given by the binomial distribution as shown in Figure 6.8.

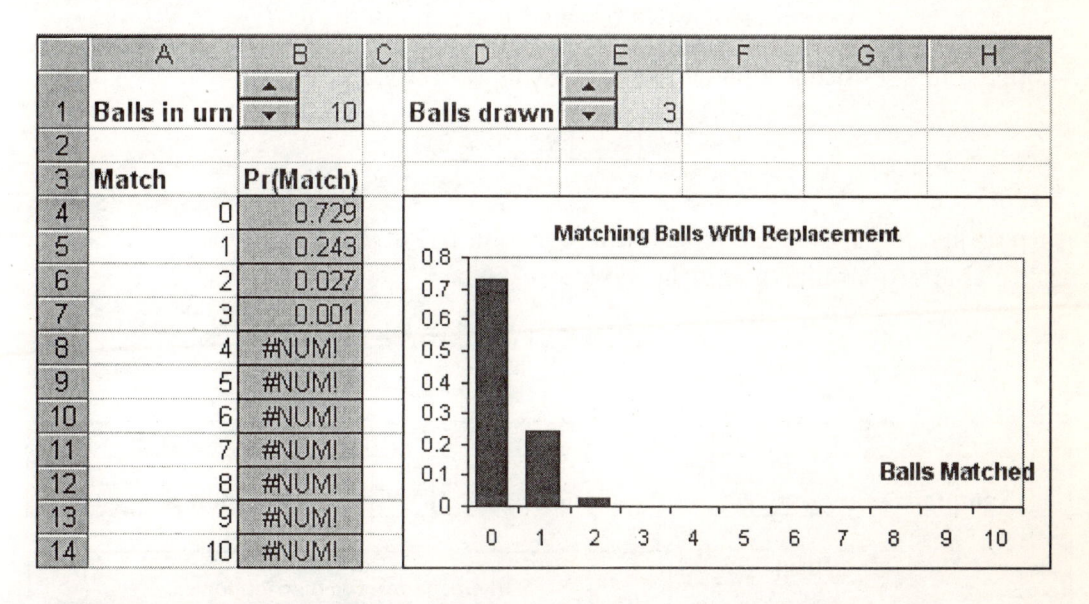

Figure 6.8: The chances of winning the Daily 3 game - a binomial distribution.

In the Texas lottery game CASH 5, players attempt to match 3, 4, or 5 numbered balls to 5 balls drawn randomly **without replacement** from an urn. For lottery games such as the Texas CASH 5, the binomial distribution does not apply. Binomial trials such those in the Daily 3 game are independent; however in CASH 5, selection of successive balls is not independent because the balls are not put back into the machine. For CASH 5, the probability of the first ball being a 1 are 1 in 39. If a 1 is selected, the probability of a 1 on the second ball is 0. If 1 is not selected on the first ball, the probability of selecting it on the second ball drops to 1 in 38 because there is one fewer ball in the machine.

CHAPTER 6. PROBABILITY DISTRIBUTIONS   120

To compute the probability of matching 3 of the numbers drawn in the Texas CASH 5, note that we have $N = 39$ numbered balls from which to choose. Of these 39, $M = 5$ are successes in the sense that they are numbered balls actually drawn from the urn. A person playing CASH 5 will select $n = 5$ numbers between 1 and 39 at random and wants to know the probability of matching $x = 3$ of the numbers. The probability of matching exactly 3 of the 5 balls drawn from the urn is

$$\frac{(\text{number of ways of getting 3 successes})(\text{number of ways of getting 2 failures})}{\text{number of ways of selecting 5 balls from 39}}.$$

In general, the probability of matching exactly x of the n balls when drawing M balls randomly from an urn of size N is given by

$$\frac{(\text{number of ways of getting } x \text{ successes})(\text{number of ways of getting } n-x \text{ failures})}{\text{number of ways of selecting } n \text{ balls from } N}.$$

By doing some counting, one can see that this probability is

$$\frac{({}_M C_x) \cdot ({}_{N-M} C_{n-x})}{{}_N C_n}.$$

With parameters x, n, M, N as given above, the HYPGEOMDIST function in *Excel* can compute this probability using the syntax

$$\texttt{=HYPGEOMDIST}(x,n,M,N)$$

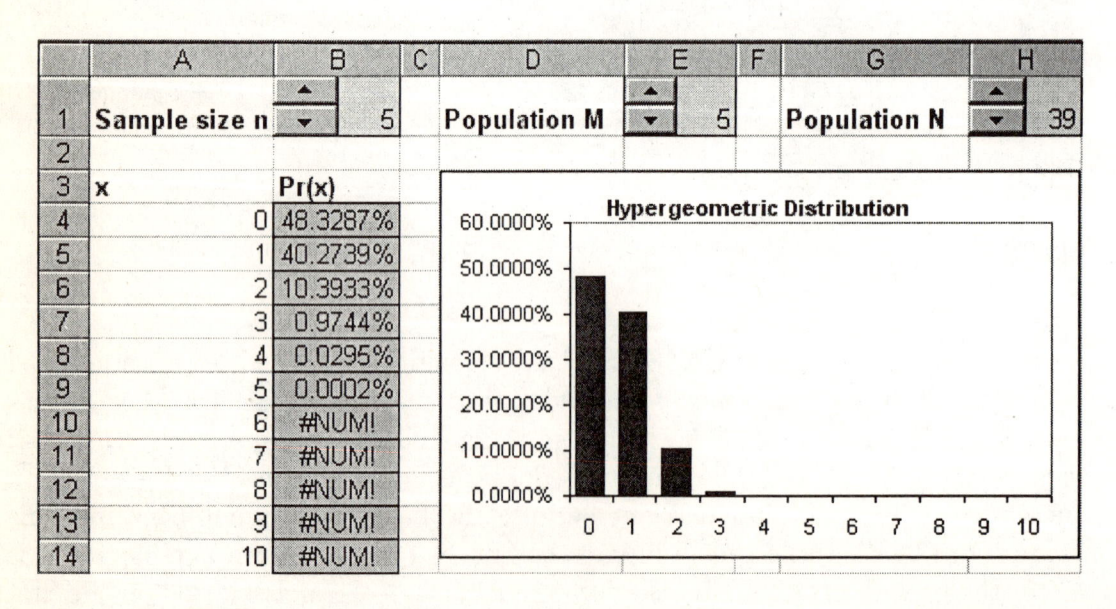

Figure 6.9: The chances of winning the CASH 5 game - a hypergeometric distribution.

CHAPTER 6. PROBABILITY DISTRIBUTIONS

Figure 6.9 illustrates how the HYPGEOMDIST function can be applied to the CASH 5 lottery game. The key formula,

$$\text{=HYPGEOMDIST(A4,\$B\$1,\$E\$1,\$H\$1)},$$

in cell B4 computes the probability of choosing 0 of the 5 numbers drawn from the 39 ball urn. This formula is then copied down column B to give the hypergeometric distribution as shown.

1. In the Wisconsin lottery's Pick 4 game, players try to match (in order) 4 balls selected with replacement from an urn containing balls labeled 0-9. What is the probability of matching all 4 numbers? Adapt the spreadsheet 'Daily 3' in the workbook HypergeometricProject.xls to determine the probability of matching 0,1,2, or 3 numbers in this game.

2. Describe how a probability distribution representing number of balls matched in a lottery game such as the Minnesota Daily 3 or the Wisconsin Pick 4 changes as the number of balls drawn from an urn containing 10 numbered balls increases.

3. Consider a lottery game in which an urn containing 2 balls has 4 balls drawn with replacement. A typical winning number might be 2122. Using the spreadsheet 'Daily 3,' describe how the probability distribution for matching x balls in such a lottery game changes as the number of balls in the urn increases.

4. In the game of Hearts involving four players, each player is dealt 13 cards from a standard 52 card deck. Alter the spreadsheet 'CASH 5' to determine the probability of a particular player receiving 5 face cards (Jack, Queen, or King) in their hand. Plot the hypergeometric distribution representing the probability of this player receiving 0,1,2,3,...12 face cards in this game.

5. Consider the hypergeometric distribution with parameters x, n, M, and N. If N is even and $M = N/2$, is there anything special we can say about the distribution. Experiment using the spreadsheet 'CASH 5' by changing the value of n in the case where $M = 6$ and $N = 12$. Then, try other values for M and N.

6. Consider again the hypergeometric distribution with parameters x, n, M, and N. If N is even, how do the distributions with $M = N/2 + 1$ and $M = N/2 - 1$ compare? Using the spreadsheet 'CASH 5,' begin your experimentation with $N = 12$.

7. Use the spreadsheet 'Simulate' to simulate playing the Texas CASH 5 game 30 times. Do you ever win the jackpot by matching all five balls drawn? Do you ever win if you simulate playing CASH 5 300 times? 3,000 times? 30,000 times?

8. To play Lotto Georgia, one selects six numbers from 1 to 46. To win, one simply matches 3,4,5, or 6 numbered balls randomly drawn without replacement from an urn. Simulate playing Lotto Georgia 1,000 times. How often are you able to match three of the six balls drawn? How often should you do this in theory?

> **You make the call:** Your state has called on you to develop a new lottery game in which 7 balls will be randomly drawn without replacement from an urn containing N balls. To win the jackpot, a player will only need to match 6 or 7 of the numbered balls drawn. Use the spreadsheet 'Simulation' to determine how large N should be taken so that the theoretical probability of winning the jackpot is less than 0.00001%. Simulate 30,000 players playing the new lottery game you've developed. Does anybody win? Is this good or bad?

CHAPTER 6. PROBABILITY DISTRIBUTIONS

6.5 The Normal Distribution

[Download: NormalProject.xls]

Because the normal distribution is associated with such a difficult function to work with by hand,
$$f(x) = \frac{1}{\sqrt{2\pi}\sigma} e^{-\frac{1}{2}\left(\frac{x-\mu}{\sigma}\right)^2},$$
Excel becomes a wonderful tool for approximating solutions to problems involving such work.

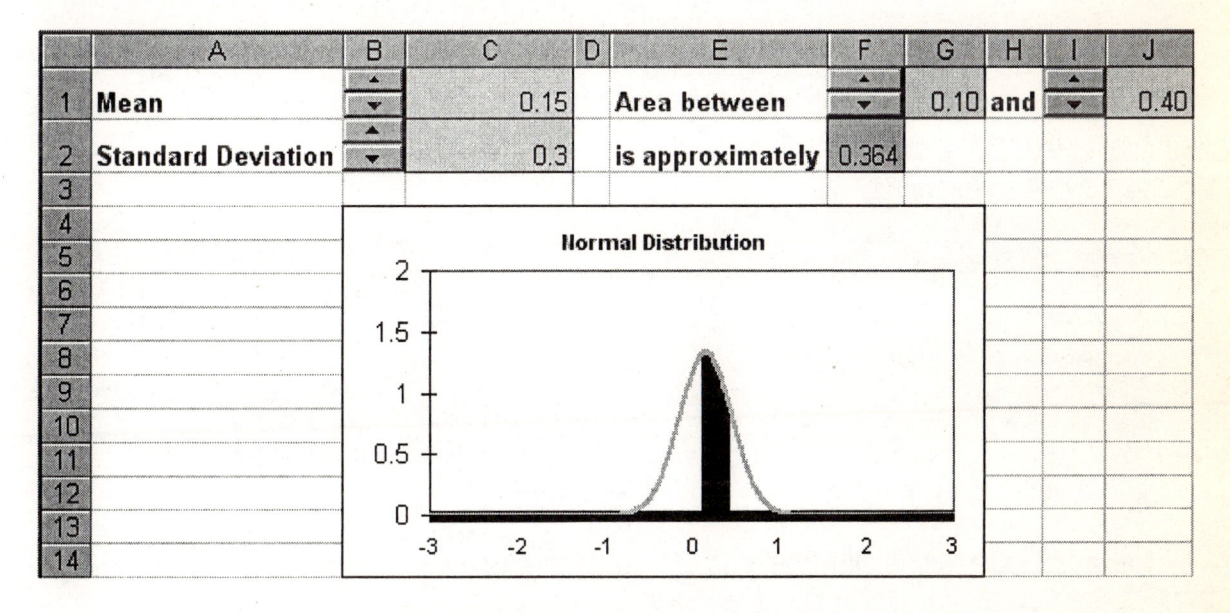

Figure 6.10: Finding area under a normal curve.

Figure 6.10 illustrates one such use with the spreadsheet 'Experiment.' For the normal distribution with mean $\mu = 0.15$ and standard deviation $\sigma = 0.3$, the area under the curve between 0.10 and 0.40 is approximately 0.364. Before the invention of electronic tools such as spreadsheets, this type of calculation was done primarily using huge tables of numbers! The key formula in this spreadsheet is

`=NORMDIST($J$1,$C$1,$C$2,TRUE)-NORMDIST($G$1,$C$1,$C$2,TRUE)`

and occurs in cell `F2`. Essentially, this formula is subtracting two areas – one is the area under the normal curve up to 0.40 and the other is the area under the curve up to 0.10. The references to cells `C1` and `C2` are simply telling *Excel* that we are interested in the normal distribution defined by a mean which occurs in cell `C1` and

CHAPTER 6. PROBABILITY DISTRIBUTIONS

by a standard deviation which occurs in cell C2. The use of the parameter TRUE is for calculating area under the curve up to that point. If we were to use the word FALSE here, *Excel* would calculate the height of the normal curve at that point instead of an area.

Another nice use of the spreadsheet is for finding the locations of percentiles for a particular normal distribution. Consider for example the **standard normal distribution** having mean $\mu = 0$ and standard deviation $\sigma = 1$. To locate the x-value corresponding to the 95% percentile of such a distribution, we can use the Goal Seek tool in *Excel*. In cell E8 of the spreadsheet 'z-scores,' we use the formula

$$\text{=NORMDIST(\$E\$4,\$C\$1,\$C\$2,TRUE)}$$

to compute the area of such a normal curve up to the value x which lies in cell E4. Under the Tools menu, we then choose Goal Seek and set the value of cell E8 to 0.95 by changing the value in cell E4. We find that about 95% of the area lies to the left of 1.64. Similarly, we could show that about 90% of the area lies to the left of 1.28.

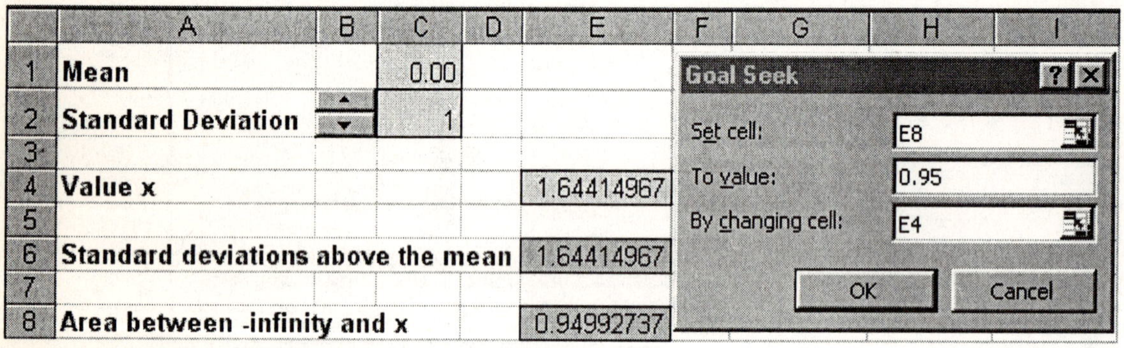

Figure 6.11: Seeking a percentage of area under a normal curve.

1. Use the spreadsheet 'Experiment' to form a hypothesis about how the normal distribution changes as the mean μ changes.

2. Use the spreadsheet 'Experiment' to form a hypothesis about how the normal distribution changes as the standard deviation σ changes.

3. Consider a normal distribution with mean $\mu = 0$ and standard deviation $\sigma = 0.7$. Use the spreadsheet 'Experiment' to compare the areas under this normal distribution between -0.2 and 0 and between 0 and 0.2. What might you conclude? Use your conclusion to compute the area under this normal curve between -0.3 and -0.2 by computing the area between 0.2 and 0.3.

CHAPTER 6. PROBABILITY DISTRIBUTIONS

4. Consider a normal distribution with mean $\mu = 0.2$ and standard deviation $\sigma = 0.4$. Use the spreadsheet 'Experiment' to determine the total area under this normal curve between $-\infty$ and 0.1 and 0.3 and ∞.

5. Consider a normal distribution with mean $\mu = 0$ and standard deviation 0.5. Use the spreadsheet 'Experiment' to determine what percentage of the area under this normal curve lies within one standard deviation of the mean. That is, between -0.5 and 0.5. How much lies within two standard deviations of the mean? three standard deviations?

6. Answer the previous question using a normal distribution having mean $\mu = 0.1$ and standard deviation 0.3. Can you form any hypothesis?

7. The value in cell E6 of the spreadsheet 'z-scores' gives the z-score corresponding the the x-value given in cell E4. The z-score is of course the number of standard deviations that x is above the mean μ, i.e. $x = \mu + z\sigma$. Use this spreadsheet to compute the z-score of $x = 3$ for a normal distribution having mean $\mu = 2.4$ and standard deviation $\sigma = 0.3$. What happens to this z-score as the standard deviation σ increases? Do you think this always happens?

8. Use the spreadsheet 'z-scores' to form a hypothesis as to what happens to a z-score as the mean *decreases*. Reason why you believe your hypothesis is always true.

9. Use the `Goal Seek` tool and the spreadsheet 'z-scores' to determine the x-value corresponding to the 75th percentile of the standard normal distribution. Then, determine the x-value corresponding to the 25th percentile of the standard normal distribution.

10. Repeat the previous problem for the 65th and 35th percentiles. Can you form any hypothesis based on these results?

11. Why is it that when using the spreadsheet 'z-scores' on the *standard normal distribution*, that the value in cell E4 is always the same as the value in cell E6. Does this happen for any other normal distribution? Explain.

> **You make the call:** For a normal distribution having mean $\mu = -1$ and standard deviation $\sigma = 0.5$, the spreadsheet 'z-scores' claims that the area under this normal curve up to the x-value 3 is 1. Is this correct? Does the z-score in cell E6 help you in making this decision?

6.6 Approximating the Binomial Distribution

[Download: ApproxProject.xls]

Imagine an experiment where Shaquille O'Neal of the Los Angeles Lakers, a 51% free throw shooter during the 2000-2001 NBA basketball season, takes 50 (independent[9]) free throws. Suppose we wanted to know how likely it is that he would make 20 or more of these. Using the binomial distribution, we would have to compute the sum

$$_{50}C_{20}(0.51)^{20}(0.49)^{30} +_{50}C_{21}(0.51)^{21}(0.49)^{29} + \ldots +_{50}C_{50}(0.51)^{50}(0.49)^0.$$

Of course, with *Excel*, this is easily done. What if, however, Shaq were to take 1,000,000 free throws? What is the probability that he would make 850,000 or more of these? Even with *Excel*, such a sum would not be fun to calculate.

But, wait a minute. We would never make Shaq take 1,000,000 free throws. That is just ridiculous. But, we just might be in the business of producing widgets. And it just might be that in the tricky production of these widgets, we have a success rate of 51%. And, it just might be that we would like to know the probability in 1,000,000 attempts that 850,000 or more of these widgets are made successfully.

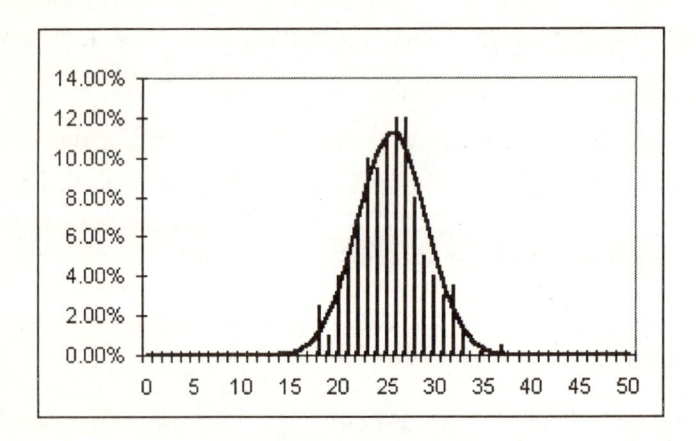

Figure 6.12: Shaq shoots 50 free throws 2000 times.

Using the spreadsheet 'Normal Approximation,' we can perform 2000 simulations of Shaq shooting 50 free throws. The results are shown in Figure 6.12. As the figure shows, the results are very nearly in a normal distribution with mean

$$\mu = (50)(0.51) = 25.5$$

---

[9]Once again, we will make the realistic assumption that these free throws are independent events and that Shaq does not get into a 'groove.'

CHAPTER 6. PROBABILITY DISTRIBUTIONS

and standard deviation
$$\sigma = \sqrt{(50)(0.51)(0.49)} \approx 3.535.$$

These values were found using the obvious formulas =G3*C1 in cell C3 and the formula =SQRT(G5*C1*(1-C1)) in cell G3 (see Figure 6.13).

	A	B	C	D	E	F	G
1	p		0.51				
2							
3	Mean		25.5		Standard Deviation		3.53482673
4							
5	Repetitions		200		Trials		50

Figure 6.13: Using the normal approximation to the binomial distribution.

Using this approximation, it becomes very easy to approximate the probability that Shaq will make 20 or more of his 50 free throw attempts. The same spreadsheet 'Normal Approximation' can compute this probability by having the user place the function

$$\texttt{=1-NORMDIST(20,C3,G3,TRUE)}$$

in any empty cell. Cells C3 and G3 contain the values of the approximating normal distribution as shown in Figure 6.13. The formula then computes the value of 1 minus the area under this normal curve between $-\infty$ and 20. Try it. You should find this probability to be approximately 94%.

1. Use the spreadsheet 'Normal Approximation' to approximate the probability that Shaq will make 25 or more of his 50 free throws. Then, use the formula =SUM(B33:B58) to compute the empirical probability that Shaq made 25 or more of his free throws during the simulation.

2. Approximate the probability that Shaq will make 15 or fewer of his 50 free throws using the NORMDIST function and the spreadsheet 'Normal Approximation.' According to the simulation, what is the empirical probability that Shaq makde 15 or fewer of his 50 free throws?

3. During the 2000-2001 NBA season, Toronto Raptor basketball player Vince Carter made approximately 76% of his free throws. Using the spreadsheet 'Normal Approximation,' Vince will make between 35 and 41 free throws out of 50 approximately what percentage of the time?

4. Using the results of the simulation, how often should you expect Vince to make 35 or more of his 50 free throws? Approximate this probability using the NORMDIST function.

5. Place the formula =1-NORMDIST(40,C3,G3,TRUE) in cell I3. Then use Goal Seek under the Tools menu to determine how good a free throw shooter must be in order to be 90% confident that they will make 40 or more of their free throws. In Goal Seek you will want to change the value in cell B1.

> **You make the call:** You are given 3-1 odds that Vince Carter, a.k.a. 76% free throw shooter will make exactly 38, 39, 40, 41, 42, or 43 free throws in 50 attempts. This means you would get $3 back for every $1 bet on this event occuring should it happen. Should you place a bet? Use the NORMDIST function in the spreadsheet 'Normal Approximation' to approximate the probability of this even occuring. Then, run one simulation of this event to see if you would win.

Chapter 7

Descriptive Statistics

7.1 Sorting Through It All

[Download: SortingProject.xls]

In the 21st century, one can find data everywhere. Sorting through all of this data can be an arduous task. A spreadsheet can help greatly in this endeavor. As a beginning example, consider the mass of data[1] in the spreadsheet '1999 Nasdaq Data.'

	A	B	C	D	E
1	Date	Composite	Volume	Advances	Declines
2	01/04/1999	2208.05	936,659,300	2,207	1,946
3	01/05/1999	2251.27	948,351,900	2,244	1,748
4	01/06/1999	2320.86	1,252,652,200	2,521	1,575
5	01/07/1999	2326.09	1,200,895,100	1,891	2,112
6	01/08/1999	2344.41	1,286,693,900	2,305	1,771
7	01/11/1999	2384.59	1,140,928,800	2,097	1,967

Figure 7.1: Sorting through a mass of Nasdaq data.

As it appears, the data is ordered according to the date. However, it may be that we are interested in ordering the data according to the volume of trading (heavy to light). To do this, we highlight all the data (cells A2 through E253) and then choose the Sort tool under the Data menu. As Figure 7.2 shows, we wish to sort Descending by Volume. One can't help but to note that the two lightest trading days were, not

---

[1] www.marketdata.nasdaq.com

CHAPTER 7. DESCRIPTIVE STATISTICS   130

suprisingly, 5/28/99 and 11/26/99. Had we not had column titles, we would use the name `Column C` rather than `Volume`. Notice how *all* of the rows are rearranged according the value that appears in column C.

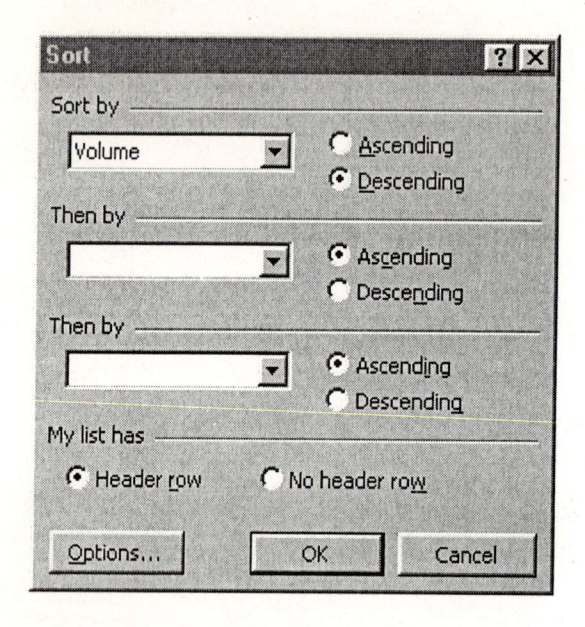

Figure 7.2: The `Sort` tool in *Excel*.

1. Use the Nasdaq data in the spreadsheet '1999 Nasdaq Data' to sort the data according to advancers. That is, the number of stocks that increased in price.

2. It appears that there is a positive correlation between the increase in the Nasdaq Composite and the number of advancers. Use *Excel* to do a `Scatter Plot` of two columns. You will need to create one of these columns which is to contain the percentage increase of the Nasdaq Composite for the day. Is there such a positive correlation? Does it matter how the data is sorted in order to do this? Explain.

> **You make the call:** Use the spreadsheet 'More 1999 Nasdaq Data' to do a `Scatter Plot` of the columns of data representing the Nasdaq Composite Index and the Nasdaq Computer Index. Is there a positive correlation? If so, find how strong it is by fitting a linear function to the data. If 'More 1999 Nasdaq Data' was sorted according to the Composite Index, how much change would you expect to see if it was subsequently sorted by the Computer Index? Why? What if the slope of the line of best fit was negative? What would that mean?

CHAPTER 7. DESCRIPTIVE STATISTICS   131

7.2 Frequency Distributions

[Download: FrequencyProject.xls]

Often a graph depicting a mass of raw data doesn't exhibit much useful information. In some of these circumstances, the use of frequency tables can nicely summarize such data.

Over the past 10 years, it seems that the stock market has been more volatile than in the past. The data in the spreadsheet 'Monthly DJIA' can be used to help us decide whether such is indeed the case.

	B	C	D	E	F	G	H
1	Month	DJIA	% Increase		Increase	Frequency	Last 10 years
2	December	235.4			less than -10%	6.0	1.0
3	January	248.8	5.69%		-10% to -5%	44.0	7.0
4	February	252.1	1.33%		-5% to 0%	200.0	32.0
5	March	247.9	-1.67%		0% to 5%	350.0	80.0
6	April	259.1	4.52%		5% to 10%	71.0	17.0
7	May	249.7	-3.63%		more than 10%	8.0	1.0

Figure 7.3: Creating class intervals for the monthly DJIA data.

To begin one possible analysis, we import monthly closing averages for the DJIA (Dow Jones Industrial Average) from December 1950 to December 2000 into a spreadsheet such as we have in 'Monthly DJIA.' Next, we compute the monthly percentage increase of the DJIA by copying the formula =C3/C2-1 down column D. It is helpful to Format these cells as a percentage.

After choosing appropriate class intervals (as shown in Figure 7.3), we can proceed to count how many months the market was up/down each percentage. To start, we place the formula

$$\text{=COUNTIF(\$D\$3:\$D\$602,"<-0.10")}$$

in cell G2 to count the number of times the market lost more than 10% in a single month. Next, in cell G3, we use the key formula

$$\text{=COUNTIF(\$D\$3:\$D\$602,"<-0.05")-COUNTIF(\$D\$3:\$D\$602,"<-0.10")}$$

and copy it down column G changing the values within the quotation marks as needed. The use of the absolute references in this formula becomes clear when we wish to repeat this process on the DJIA monthly data from the past 10 years. We simply

CHAPTER 7. DESCRIPTIVE STATISTICS 132

copy the formulas from cells G2 through G7 to cells H2 through H7. In each of these cells, the only item that needs changing in each COUNTIF function is $D$3 which becomes $D$483. Plotting the information from cells F2 through H7 in the form of a bar graph gives a frequency chart as shown in Figure 7.4.

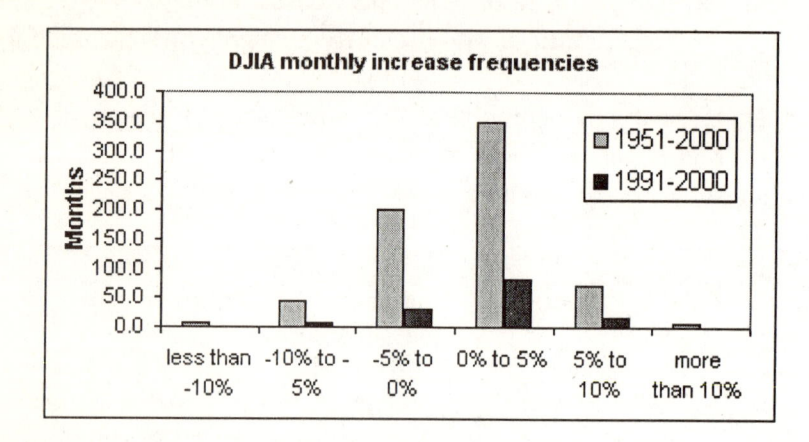

Figure 7.4: Comparing historical monthly increases in the DJIA.

The chart in Figure 7.4 is still not what we are really looking for. It is difficult to tell from this chart whether the market has been more volatile in the past 10 years because we are not looking at *relative* frequencies. To make a better comparison, we create another table in the spreadsheet (see Figure 7.5) using the table of information we have already created.

	F	G	H
9	Increase	Rel. Freq.	Last 10 years
10	less than -10%	0.9%	0.7%
11	-10% to -5%	6.5%	5.1%
12	-5% to 0%	29.5%	23.2%
13	0% to 5%	51.5%	58.0%
14	5% to 10%	10.5%	12.3%
15	more than 10%	1.2%	0.7%

Figure 7.5: Creating a relative frequency chart from a frequency chart.

The formula, =G2/SUM(G$2:G$7) occurring in cell G10 is the key to this process. Through a keen use of $'s, this formula can now be copied to the rest of the cells in the grid G10 through H15 to compute the relative frequency of each monthly percentage increase in the DJIA. A bar graph of the relative frequency data is shown in Figure 7.6.

CHAPTER 7. DESCRIPTIVE STATISTICS 133

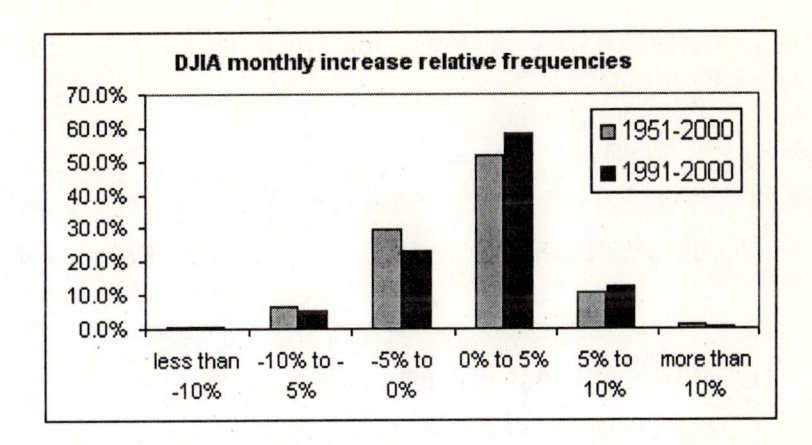

Figure 7.6: Yet another comparison of historical monthly increases in the DJIA.

One other often quoted fact is that of the stock market having a January 'bounce' and poorly performing in October. Using the monthly DJIA data and the `Sort` command found under the `Data` menu, we can decide for ourselves. To sort the data according to month, we highlight cells `A2` through `D601` and `Sort` by column B. This will put the data in alphabetical order according to column B. To put it in the natural monthly order, we use the `Options` on the `Sort` tool.

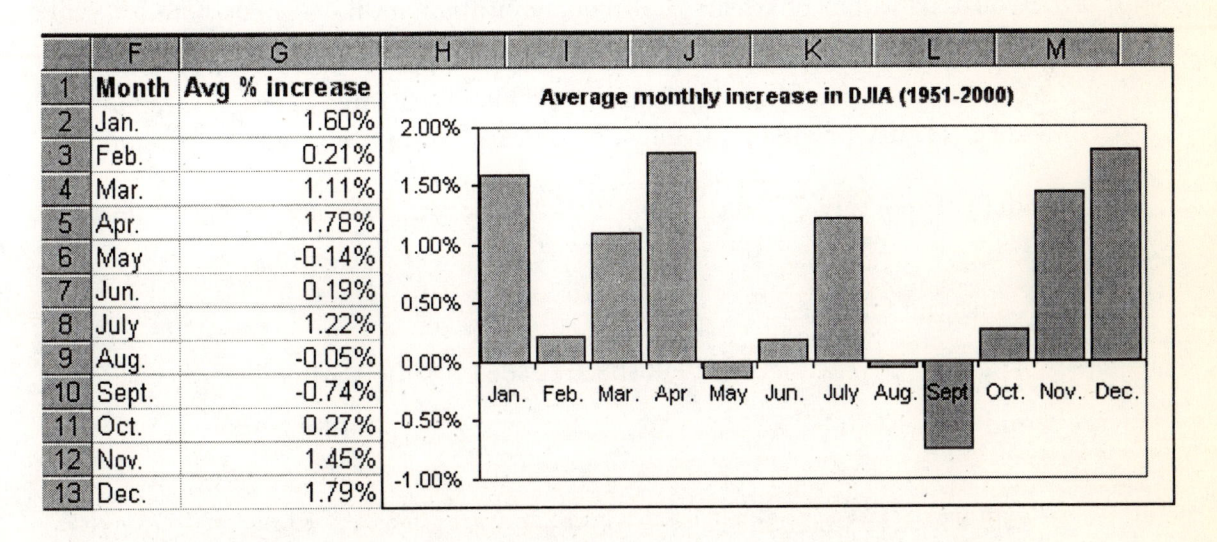

Month	Avg % increase
Jan.	1.60%
Feb.	0.21%
Mar.	1.11%
Apr.	1.78%
May	-0.14%
Jun.	0.19%
July	1.22%
Aug.	-0.05%
Sept.	-0.74%
Oct.	0.27%
Nov.	1.45%
Dec.	1.79%

Figure 7.7: Average monthly increase in the DJIA by month.

1. Consider the presidential data contained in the spreadsheet 'Presidential Data' of the workbook `FrequencyProject.xls`. For this particular data, it appears natural that 6 class intervals having a width of 10 years will nicely summarize

CHAPTER 7. DESCRIPTIVE STATISTICS 134

the data. The choice of these intervals along with the corresponding frequencies are shown in Figure 7.8.

(a) Use *Excel's* COUNTIF command to contruct the frequencies in column E of this spreadsheet. *Hint:* In cell E3, try the formula

=COUNTIF(B$3:B$38,">=40")-COUNTIF(B$3:B$38,">=50").

	A	B	C	D	E
1	President	Age at death		Class	Frequency
2					
3	Washington	67		40-49	2
4	Adams	60		50-59	5
5	Jefferson	83		60-69	13
6	Madison	85		70-79	10
7	Monroe	73		80-89	5
8	Adams	80		90-99	1
		78			

Figure 7.8: Constructing class intervals for the presidential data.

(b) Construct a bar chart for the frequency table you have constructed.

(c) How do 20th century presidential lifespans compare to previous presidents? Create a relative frequency bar chart which illustrates how the lifespans of 20th century presidents (McKinley onward) compare to all the presidents.

2. Consider the monthly CPI data from 1946-2000 given in the spreadsheet 'Monthly CPI.'

(a) Using the formulas

=COUNTIF($D$3:$D$661,"<-0.01")

and

=COUNTIF($D$3:$D$661,"<-0.005")-COUNTIF($D$3:$D$661,"<-0.010")

given in cells G2 and G3 respectively as a guide, use the COUNTIF function to fill in the frequency table as shown in Figure 7.9.

CHAPTER 7. DESCRIPTIVE STATISTICS

	F	G	H
1	Increase	Frequency	1971-1980
2	less than -1.0%	0.0	0.0
3	-1.0% to -0.5%	8.0	0.0
4	-0.5% to 0%	34.0	0.0
5	0% to 0.5%	445.0	50.0
6	0.5% to 1.0%	129.0	48.0
7	1.0% to 1.5%	33.0	20.0
8	more than 1.5%	10.0	2.0

Figure 7.9: Constructing class intervals for the monthly CPI data.

(b) Create a relative frequency table corresponding to the frequency table of Figure 7.9. Construct a bar chart for this relative frequency table. For those who claim that inflation (as measured by the CPI) was worse in the 1970's than other recent periods, what does your chart suggest?

3. Use the spreadsheet 'Monthly Mortgage Rates' containing historical 30-year conventional loan data to create a frequency table having class intervals 6-7%, 7-8%, 8-9%, 9-10%, 10-11%, and over 11%. Then, plot this frequency table in the form of a bar graph. Are current 30-year rates pretty good for the consumer from a historical perspective?

CHAPTER 7. DESCRIPTIVE STATISTICS 136

You make the call: A friend of yours claims that February is the best time of the year to take out a conventional 30-year loan to buy a house. As proof, she shows you the chart in Figure 7.10. Use the spreadsheet 'More Monthly Mortgage Rates' containing historical rate data to verify that your friend is correct by reproducing such a chart. Then, decide what month of the year you might want to buy your own home.

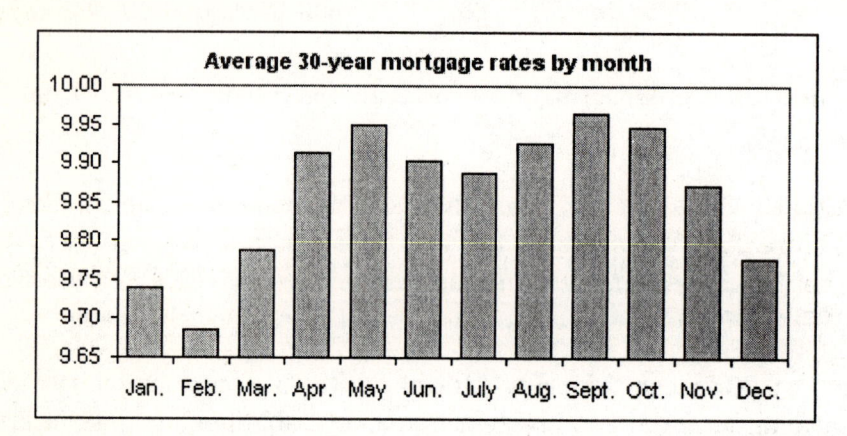

Figure 7.10: Chart showing when to take out a 30-year conventional mortgage.

CHAPTER 7. DESCRIPTIVE STATISTICS 137

7.3 Sizing up a Data Set

[Download: MutualFundProject.xls]

The 134 equity mutual funds listed in the spreadsheet 'Businessweek A Funds' are Businessweek's picks[2] for delivering the best risk-adjusted total returns over the past five years. For this data, there are several ways in which we could measure how a particular mutual fund on this list stacks up against the others. For example, perhaps the easiest and most common measure would be to compute the **average**, i.e. **mean**, return of all the funds. In *Excel*, there is a built-in function AVERAGE that will do this for us.

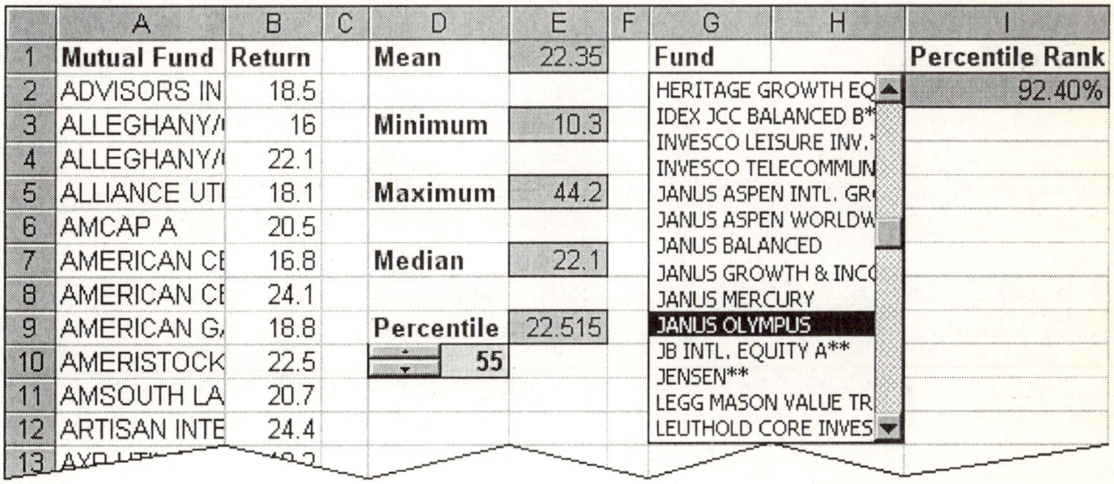

Figure 7.11: Comparing a list of mutual funds according to average return.

Of course, there are other methods of measuring the location of a data set such as the **median**, **mode**, **minimum**, **maximum**, and **percentiles**. For a given data set, all of these values can be found easily using *Excel*. To compute the mean, minimum, maximum, and percentiles of the numerical data found in cells B2 through B135 of the spreadsheet as shown in Figure 7.11, we use the formulas as given in the chart below.

Mean	=AVERAGE(B2:B135)
Minimum	=MIN(B2:B135)
Maximum	=MAX(B2:B135)
Percentile	=PERCENTILE(B2:B135,D10/100)

[2]Source: www.Businessweek.com, January 29, 2001

CHAPTER 7. DESCRIPTIVE STATISTICS   138

In a data set such as Businessweek's A fund list, we are sometimes also interested in determining the percentile rank of a particular item in the list. For example, in our list we may be interested in investing in the Janus Olympus fund and would like to know how it stacks up on Businessweek's list as far as return is concerned. For such a purpose, *Excel* has a function called PERCENTRANK. To use it, we find which cell the return for the Janus Olympus fund is located (B61) and use the syntax =PERCENTRANK(B2:B135,B61).[3] As Figure 7.11 illustrates, the average annual return on this fund is higher than 92.4% of the others on this list.

1. Using the spreadsheet 'Businessweek A Funds,' find the **mode** (most common element) of the average annual returns in Businessweek's list. To do this, you will need to use the MODE function built into *Excel*. Try to figure out what parameters you need to enter into the MODE function on your own!

2. The spreadsheet 'Family Median Income' contains data for the median 4-person family income for 1998 by state according to the U.S. Census Bureau.

    (a) Using the MEDIAN function, compute the median 1998 statewide median 4-person family income.

    (b) Use the MIN and MAX functions to compute the maximum and minimum statewide 1998 median family income.

    (c) Using the PERCENTILE function, compute the 1998 statewide median family income at the 75th percentile. Use the COUNTIF command to count how many states had median family incomes above this level. Does your answer make sense?

    (d) The state of North Dakota had a median family income of $51,002 during 1998. Using the PERCENTRANK function, compute the percentile that North Dakota ranks in median family income. Do the same for your state.

3. The spreadsheet 'NBA Scoring 2000-01' contains the total number of minutes played and points scored for 441 NBA players during the 2000-01 regular season.[4]

    (a) Using the AVERAGE and MEDIAN functions, compute and compare the mean and median number of points scored per player in the NBA during the 2000-01 regular season. Discuss.

    (b) Use the MAX function to compute how many points the season scoring leader posted.

---

[3]To have output such as shown in Figure 7.11, the user would need to use the Forms toolbar and the INDEX function.

[4]Source: www.allsports.com

(c) Insert a new column D and use it to find the maximum number of points scored per minute played.

(d) Use to Sort tool under the Data menu to sort the data according to number of points scored with the maximum number listed first.

(e) For settling a contract, players may wish to know if they were in the top 10% in scoring during the season. How many points would one need to score in order to be in the 90th percentile according to this data? Use the COUNTIF function to determine how many players scored more than this number of points. Does your answer make sense?

> **You make the call:** Partial results of the 1999 National Occupational Employment Statistics Survey[5] are given in the spreadsheet '1999 OES Wage Statistics.' The spreadsheet shows average annual salaries for 709 chosen occupations. Use this information and the power of *Excel* to compute the maximum, minimum, and median salary surveyed. To be an occupation in the top 10% of this list, what average annual salary is required? At what percentile do accountants and auditors rank? How about legislators?

7.4 Measuring Spread

[Download: StandardDeviationProject.xls]

Besides measuring the location of a particular data set, we are also often interested in measuring how spread out the values in a data set are. Consider the data shown in Figure 7.12 representing the high and low temperatures for Minneapolis-St. Paul from May 4, 2001 to May 23, 2001.[6]

	A	B	C	D	E	F	G
1	Day	High Temp	Low Temp		Day	High Temp	Low Temp
2	04-May-01	64	50		14-May-01	94	55
3	05-May-01	57	51		15-May-01	94	70
4	06-May-01	68	53		16-May-01	78	61
5	07-May-01	64	48		17-May-01	77	55
6	08-May-01	66	49		18-May-01	76	52
7	09-May-01	76	49		19-May-01	79	56
8	10-May-01	68	52		20-May-01	65	54
9	11-May-01	63	48		21-May-01	62	47
10	12-May-01	67	43		22-May-01	47	39
11	13-May-01	73	50		23-May-01	52	36

Figure 7.12: High and Low temperature data for Minneapolis-St. Paul.

A quick glimse at the data or at Figure 7.12 shows that the high temperatures during the period from May 14 to May 23 were much more varied than those during the period from May 4 to May 13. The same variance is even more pronouced for the corresponding lows.

There are various methods by which we can measure just how much this data is spread out. The first is a very simple measure called the **range**. One possible formula which would calculate the range of high temperatures between May 4, 2001 and May 13, 2001 is given by

$$\text{=MAX(B2:B11)-MIN(B2:B11)}$$

Another method of computation would be to substract the 0th percentile from the 100th percentile as exhibited by

$$\text{=PERCENTILE(B2:B11,1)-PERCENTILE(B2:B11,0)}.$$

---
[6]Source: National Weather Service

CHAPTER 7. DESCRIPTIVE STATISTICS

In this example, it is easy to see that the range of high temperatures between May 4 and May 13 is 19 degrees while the range for the next 10-day period is a whopping 47 degrees!

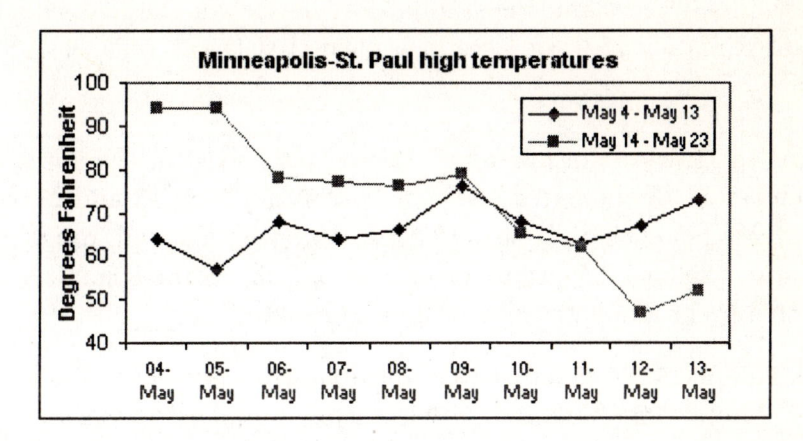

Figure 7.13: Difference in high temperature data for Minneapolis-St. Paul (May 4, 2001 – May 13, 2001 vs. May 14, 2001 – May 23).

In general, since the range is a poor measure of spread for large sets of data due to the effects of **outliers**, we tend to use other measures of spread more commonly. One such is called the **Interquartile range**. The interquartile range (IQR) is the difference between the 75th percentile and the 25th percentile. Note that we are simply measuring the inside two quarters of the range. To calculate the interquartile range of high temperatures between May 4 and May 13, we could use the formula

=PERCENTILE(B2:B11,0.75)-PERCENTILE(B2:B11,0.25).

A third measure of spread commonly used is the **standard deviation**. There are two types of standard deviation. There is the **standard deviation s of a sample** and the **standard deviation σ of a population**. If the set $\{x_1, x_2, \ldots, x_n\}$ is a set of n sample measurements with mean $\bar{x}$, then

$$s = \sqrt{\frac{(x_1 - \bar{x})^2 + (x_2 - \bar{x})^2 + \ldots + (x_n - \bar{x})^2}{n - 1}}.$$

If the set $\{x_1, x_2, \ldots, x_n\}$ is a whole population with mean μ, then

$$\sigma = \sqrt{\frac{(x_1 - \mu)^2 + (x_2 - \mu)^2 + \ldots + (x_n - \mu)^2}{n}}.$$

In the case of the high temperature data, even though one would never measure the spread of such a small data set in practice, we will consider each set of 10 high

CHAPTER 7. DESCRIPTIVE STATISTICS 142

temperatures to be a population. Hence, to compute the standard deviation σ of the high temperatures between May 4 and May 13, we use the formula =STDEVP(B2:B11).[7] Since the standard deviation of the high temperatures between May 4 and May 13 is approximately 5.02 degrees and the standard deviation for the highs during the next 10 days is approximately 15.05 degrees, it is clear that the second set of highs is more 'spread out.'

1. Consider the two sets of low temperature data given in the spreadsheet 'Mpls Weather Data' for the dates between May 4 and May 13 and between May 14 and May 23. For each of these data sets, compute the mean, range, interquartile range, and standard deviation. Which set of temperatures is more 'spread out?' Verify this by producing a plot similar to Figure 7.13.

2. Use the PERCENTRANK function to determine what percent of high temperatures between May 4 and May 13 are within one standard deviation of the mean. within two standard deviations?

3. Consider the data set found in the spreadsheet 'NBA scoring 2000-2001.' Use this to determine the mean and standard deviation for points scored during the 2000-01 season. Interpret the result.

4. Compute the standard deviation for minutes played during the 2000-01 season. Is the points scored or minutes played data more 'spread out?'

> **You make the call:** Consider the salary data in the spreadsheet '1999 OES Salary Statistics.' Compute the mean and standard deviation for this data set and interpret the meaning of these numbers. What percent of the average annual salaries lie within one standard deviation of the mean?

---

[7]Had we considered the data set to be a sample from a larger data set, we would have used the function STDEV.

CHAPTER 7. DESCRIPTIVE STATISTICS 143

7.5 Some Theory

[Download: SomeTheoryProject.xls]

If a given data set is modified, how does that modification change the mean, median, mode, standard deviation, range, etc...? With some experimentation and the workbook `SomeTheoryProject.xls`, we can form some hypotheses.

To begin, we will consider a (random) data set with 10 elements. What happens when we add a constant amount to each element in the set? How does the mean change for example? According the the spreadsheet 'Adding a Constant' as shown in Figure 7.14, we hypothesize that the mean changes by exactly the same amount that each element in the data set changes. Similarly, we would guess that the median changes in the exact same fashion.

Data	Modified Data	Add	10
23	33		
37	47		
78	88	Change Data Set	
4	14		
95	105		
60	70		
14	24		
2	12		
8	18		
28	38		
Mean			
34.9	44.9		

Figure 7.14: How the mean of a data set changes when adding a constant amount to each element.

1. Use the spreadsheet 'Adding a Constant' to hypothesize how the *mode* of a data set changes when we add a constant to every element in that set.

2. Use the spreadsheet 'Adding a Constant' to hypothesize how the *standard deviation* of a data set changes when we add a constant to every element in that set.

3. Use the spreadsheet 'Adding a Constant' to hypothesize how the *range* of a data set changes when we add a constant to every element in that set. How about the interquartile range?

4. Use the spreadsheet 'Adding a Percent' to hypothesize how the mean, median, mode, standard deviation, range, and interquartile range change when we add a constant *percentage* to every element in that set.

> **You make the call:** Use the spreadsheet 'Doing Both' to hypothesize how the mean, median, mode, standard deviation, range, and interquartile range change when we add a constant percentage r and *then* a different constant c to every element in that set.

Chapter 8

Game Theory

8.1 Strictly Determined Games

[Download: StrictlyDeterminedGamesProject.xls]

Many of the computations involved in strictly determined games are tedious. With the workbook `StrictlyDeterminedGamesProject.xls`, we can quickly consider many examples of strictly determined games in order to form some hypotheses.

Consider first a question about a matrix game in which there are four **saddle points** as shown in Figure 8.1. What will happen to the saddle points when one of the values of the saddle points is changed? To answer this question, we begin by putting the matrix game in cells `C3` through `F6` of the spreadsheet. By clicking on the FIND STRATEGY button, this spreadsheet will do the following.

- Find the minimum row values and highlight them in blue.

- Find the maximum column values and highlight them in yellow.

- Find any saddle values and highlight them in, naturally, green.

	A	B	C	D	E	F	G	H	I	J
1			X1	X2	X3	X4	X5			
2										
3	Y1		0	-1	-1	4				
4	Y2		1	2	1	4			Find Strategy	
5	Y3		-2	0	1	1				
6	Y4		1	2	1	3				

Figure 8.1: Finding saddle points in a strictly determined game.

CHAPTER 8. GAME THEORY

We can then make changes to any saddle point we wish and let the spreadsheet recalculate. For example, suppose we wish to change the '1' in the fourth row and third column to a value of '1.5.' Recalculating gives the result seen in Figure 8.2. Notice that two of the saddle points (those in the third column) have vanished.

0	-1	-1	4
1	2	1	4
-2	0	1	1
1	2	1.5	3

Figure 8.2: Experimenting with saddle points in a strictly determined game.

Next, suppose we wish to change the '1' in the fourth row and third column to a value of '0.5.' Recalculating gives the result seen in Figure 8.3. Notice that now a different pair of the saddle points (those in the fourth row) have vanished.

0	-1	-1	4
1	2	1	4
-2	0	1	1
1	2	0.5	3

Figure 8.3: More experimenting with saddle points in a strictly determined game.

One *hypothesis* a person could form after a little more experimentation would be that once the value of one saddle point is increased so as to no longer be a saddle point, then all other saddle points in its column also vanish. Similarly, if the value of one saddle point is decreased so as to no longer be a saddle point, then all other saddle points in its row also vanish.

1. Use the spreadsheet 'Finding Saddle Points' to verify that the hypothesis above holds true for the game matrix

$$\begin{bmatrix} 2 & 1 & 3 \\ 4 & 6 & 4 \\ 4 & 8 & 4 \end{bmatrix}$$

by increasing and decreasing the value in the second row and first column.

2. Is it possible to change a value in a game matrix so as to change it from one having a unique saddle point to one having multiple saddle points? Experiment

CHAPTER 8. GAME THEORY

with changing the value in the third row and first column of the game matrix

$$\begin{bmatrix} 2 & 1 & 3 \\ 3 & 6 & 4 \\ 2 & 8 & 3 \end{bmatrix}.$$

3. Is it possible to change a single value in a game matrix so as to change it from having no saddle points to one having multiple saddle points? Experiment with changing the value in the third row and fourth column of the game matrix

$$\begin{bmatrix} 1 & -1 & 1 & 1 \\ 0 & 2 & 0 & 2 \\ 1 & 3 & 1 & -1 \end{bmatrix}.$$

4. Use the spreadsheet 'Finding Saddle Points' to find a game matrix having exactly three saddle points.

> **You make the call:** The child's game 'Rock, Scissors, Paper' can be considered to have game matrix
>
> $$\begin{bmatrix} 0 & -1 & 1 \\ 1 & 0 & -1 \\ -1 & 1 & 0 \end{bmatrix}.$$
>
> Use the spreadsheet 'Finding Saddle Points' to show that such a matrix has no saddle points. This matrix is also an example of a **circulant matrix** (see section 2.3). Use this spreadsheet to experiment and then form a hypothesis regarding the relationship between circulant matrices and saddle points.

CHAPTER 8. GAME THEORY   148

8.2 Rock, Scissors, Paper

[Download: RockScissorsPaperProject.xls]

Though usually not for money, the nonstrictly determined matrix game 'Rock, Scissors, Paper' as shown in Figure 8.4 is played by children all over the world.

	A	B	C	D	E	F	G	H	I	J	K	L
1			Rock	Scissors	Paper							
2												
3	Rock		0	1	-1		Find Strategy			
4	Scissors		-1	0	1				
5	Paper		1	-1	0				
6												
7	Row Player			Rock		Scissors		Paper		P		
8	Strategy			50.0%		0.0%		50.0%		0.50	0.00	0.50
9												
10	Column Player			Rock		Scissors		Paper		Q		
11	Strategy			0.00%		50.00%		50.0%		0.00		
12											0.50		
13	Value of Game		-0.2500							0.50		

Figure 8.4: The matrix game 'Rock, Scissors, Paper.'

The spreadsheet 'Rock, Paper, Scissors' allows us to experiment with different row and column strategies. Figure 8.4 shows that if the row player chooses rock half the time and paper half the time and if the column player chooses scissors half the time and paper half the time, the result is a game with a value of -0.25. This means that on average, the row player should expect to lose 25% of the time. To compute this value using *Excel* is easy with the MMULT function. In Figure 8.4, the only formula used is

$$\text{=MMULT(MMULT(J8:L8,C3:E5),J11:J13)}$$

which appears in cell C13. It simply computes the matrix product PAQ where A is the game matrix and P and Q are as in Figure 8.4.

1. Develop row and column strategies for the matrix game Rock, Scissors, Paper for which the row player should expect to *win* 25% of the time.

2. Suppose that the column player decides to use a strategy of choosing scissors half the time and paper half the time and that the row player knows this.

CHAPTER 8. GAME THEORY   149

Experiment with different row strategies using the spreadsheet 'Rock, Scissors, Paper' to determine how the row player should play. Defend your answer from a logical point of view.

3. Suppose that the column player decides to use a strategy of choosing rock 33% the time, scissors 33% of the time, and paper 34% of the time and that the row player knows this. Experiment with different row strategies using the spreadsheet 'Rock, Scissors, Paper' to determine how the row player should play.

You make the call: Suppose that when rock 'kills' scissors, it is given a weight of 2 rather than 1 as shown in Figure 8.5.

	Rock	Scissors	Paper
Rock	0	2	-1
Scissors	-2	0	1
Paper	1	-1	0

Figure 8.5: A variation of the matrix game 'Rock, Scissors, Paper.'

Suppose also that the column player decides to use a strategy of choosing rock 33% the time, scissors 33% of the time, and paper 34% of the time and that the row player knows this. Experiment with different row strategies using the spreadsheet 'Rock, Scissors, Paper' to determine how the row player should play. Does your answer make sense?

8.3 Let's Add Dynamite

[Download: DynamiteProject.xls]

The matrix game 'Rock, Scissors, Paper, Dynamite' as shown in Figure 8.6 is not a strictly determined game. However, the **Fundamental Theorem of Game Theory** tells us that each player has an optimal strategy. We will use *Excel* to help us implement a process for determining these strategies.

	Rock	Scissors	Paper	Dynamite
Rock	0	1	0	-1
Scissors	-1	0	1	0
Paper	0	-1	0	1
Dynamite	1	0	-1	0

Figure 8.6: The matrix game 'Rock, Scissors, Paper, Dynamite.'

Before we proceed, we would like our game matrix to be positive. One way to do this is to add 2 to every value in the matrix. The resulting game matrix is shown in Figure 8.7.

To begin, we determine an optimal strategy for the column player. We will solve the required maximization problem

$$\begin{aligned}
\text{Maximize} \quad & y = \tfrac{1}{v} = y_1 + y_2 + y_3 + y_4 \\
\text{subject to} \quad & 2y_1 + 3y_2 + 2y_3 + 1y_4 \leq 1 \\
& 1y_1 + 2y_2 + 3y_3 + 2y_4 \leq 1 \\
& 2y_1 + 1y_2 + 2y_3 + 3y_4 \leq 1 \\
& 3y_1 + 2y_2 + 1y_3 + 2y_4 \leq 1 \\
& y_i \geq 0 \ (i = 1, 2, 3, 4)
\end{aligned}$$

using the simplex method built into the spreadsheet 'Column Player' of the workbook `StrategyProject.xls` as we did in chapter 4.

CHAPTER 8. GAME THEORY

	A	B	C	D	E	F	G	H	I	J	K	L
1			Rock	Scissors	Paper	Dynamite						
2												
3	Rock		2	3	2	1						
4	Scissors		1	2	3	2		Find Strategy				
5	Paper		2	1	2	3						
6	Dynamite		3	2	1	2						
7												
8	Row Player		Rock	Scissors	Paper	Dynamite	S1	S2	S3	S4	Z	RHS
9												
10	Pivot on		2	3	2	1	1	0	0	0	0	1
11	selected		1	2	3	2	0	1	0	0	0	1
12	cell		2	1	2	3	0	0	1	0	0	1
13			3	2	1	2	0	0	0	1	0	1
14			-1	-1	-1	-1	0	0	0	0	1	0

Figure 8.7: Determining an optimal strategy for the column player in the matrix game 'Rock, Scissors, Paper, Dynamite.'

The solution by such a process is

$$y_1 = 0.25, \quad y_2 = 0, \quad y_3 = 0.25, \quad y_4 = 0.$$

The expected value v of this adjusted game is then given by

$$v = \frac{1}{y_1 + y_2 + y_3 + y_4} = 2.$$

An optimal column strategy is given by

$$Q_{opt} = \begin{bmatrix} vy_1 \\ vy_2 \\ vy_3 \\ vy_4 \end{bmatrix} = \begin{bmatrix} 0.5 \\ 0 \\ 0.5 \\ 0 \end{bmatrix}.$$

This means that the column player should choose rock 50% of the time, paper 50% of the time, and should never choose scissors or dynamite. Since $v = 2$, we see that the expected value of the *original* game is 0.

Next, we determine an optimal strategy for the row player. To do this, we solve

CHAPTER 8. GAME THEORY 152

the minimization problem

$$\text{Minimize} \quad y = \frac{1}{v} = x_1 + x_2 + x_3 + x_4$$
$$\text{subject to} \quad 2x_1 + 1x_2 + 2x_3 + 3x_4 \geq 1$$
$$3x_1 + 2x_2 + 1x_3 + 2x_4 \geq 1$$
$$2x_1 + 3x_2 + 2x_3 + 1x_4 \geq 1$$
$$1x_1 + 2x_2 + 3x_3 + 2x_4 \geq 1$$
$$x_i \geq 0 \quad (i = 1, 2, 3, 4)$$

	A	B	C	D	E	F
1			Rock	Scissors	Paper	Dynamite
2						
3	Rock		2	3	2	1
4	Scissors		1	2	3	2
5	Paper		2	1	2	3
6	Dynamite		3	2	1	2
7						
8	x_1		0.25	0.5	vx_1	
9	x_2		0	0	vx_2	
10	x_3		0.25	0.5	vx_3	
11	x_4		0	0	vx_4	
12						
13	y		0.5	2	v	
14						
15	Constraints					
16		1				
17		1				
18		1				
19		1				

Figure 8.8: Using *Excel's* Solver to find an optimal row strategy.

To solve the optimization problem this time, we will put the necessary information into *Excel's* Solver as was done in chapter 3. To do this, we place initial values for x_1, x_2, x_3, and x_4 in cells C8 through C11 of the spreadsheet 'Row Player' as shown in Figure 8.8. Then, in cell C13, we put the formula =SUM(C8:C11) for our objective function. In cells A16 through A19 respectively, we enter the following formulas which describe the four constraints

=C3*C8+C4*C9+C5*C10+C6*C11,
=D3*C8+D4*C9+D5*C10+D6*C11,

CHAPTER 8. GAME THEORY

=E3*C8+E4*C9+E5*C10+E6*C11, and
=F3*C8+F4*C9+F5*C10+F6*C11.

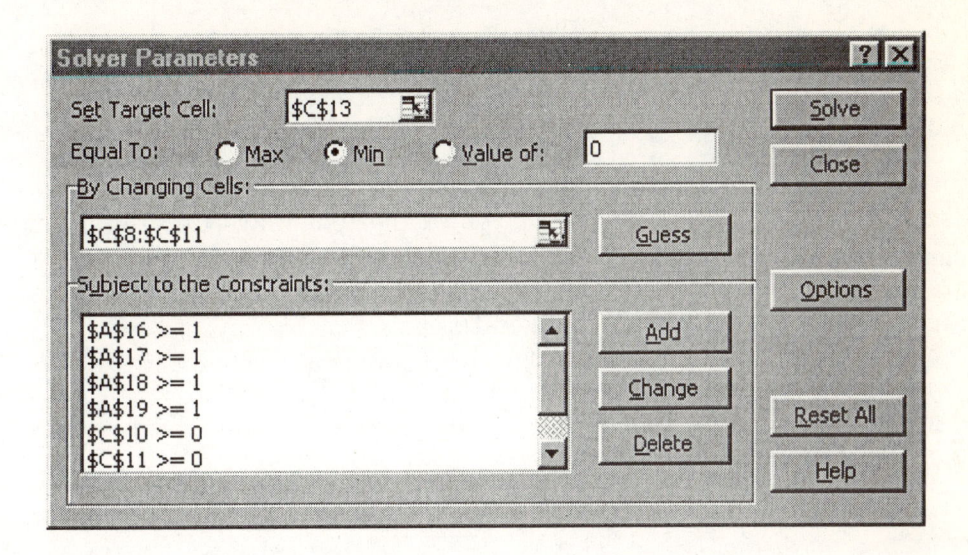

Figure 8.9: Using *Excel's* Solver to find an optimal row strategy.

Selecting the Solver under the Tools menu, we set the target cell C13 to a minimum by changing the values in the range C8:C11 subject to the constraints A16>=1, A17>=1, A18>=1, A19>=1, C8>=0, C9>=0, C10>=0, and C11>=0 as shown in Figure 8.9.

The solution by such a process is

$$x_1 = 0.25, \; x_2 = 0, \; x_3 = 0.25, \; x_4 = 0.$$

The expected value v of the game (which we also obviously compute with *Excel*) is then given by

$$v = \frac{1}{x_1 + x_2 + x_3 + x_4} = 2.$$

An optimal row strategy is given by

$$P_{opt} = \begin{bmatrix} vx_1 & vx_2 & vx_3 & vx_4 \end{bmatrix} = \begin{bmatrix} 0.5 & 0 & 0.5 & 0 \end{bmatrix}.$$

This means that the row player should choose rock 50% of the time, paper 50% of the time, and should never choose scissors or dynamite.

As an easy check, note that

$$P_{opt} \cdot A \cdot Q_{opt} = \begin{bmatrix} 0.5 & 0 & 0.5 & 0 \end{bmatrix} \begin{bmatrix} 2 & 3 & 2 & 1 \\ 1 & 2 & 3 & 2 \\ 2 & 1 & 2 & 3 \\ 3 & 2 & 1 & 2 \end{bmatrix} \begin{bmatrix} 0.5 \\ 0 \\ 0.5 \\ 0 \end{bmatrix} = 2.$$

CHAPTER 8. GAME THEORY 154

1. In an effort to make this game more interesting and have each player choose scissors more often, suppose the game matrix is changed to

$$\begin{bmatrix} 2 & 3 & 2 & 1 \\ 1 & 2 & 3.5 & 2 \\ 2 & 0.5 & 2 & 3 \\ 3 & 2 & 1 & 2 \end{bmatrix}.$$

    Use the spreadsheets 'Column Player' and 'Row Player' to determine what effects on optimal strategies this has. Are you surprised?

2. Suppose the game matrix is changed to

$$\begin{bmatrix} 2 & 3 & 2 & 0.4 \\ 1 & 2 & 3.2 & 2 \\ 2 & 0.8 & 2 & 3.4 \\ 3.6 & 2 & 0.6 & 2 \end{bmatrix}.$$

    Use the spreadsheets 'Column Player' and 'Row Player' to determine what effects on optimal strategies this has. Do your answers surprise you? Can you find more than one optimal strategy for the column player?

3. Attempt to change the game matrix in such a way that an optimal strategy would be for each player to choose Rock, Scissors, Paper, or Dynamite one-fourth of the time. Use the spreadsheets 'Column Player' and 'Row Player' to do the experimentation.

> **You make the call:** Consider the Rock, Scissors, Paper, Dynamite game in which the game matrix is given by
>
> $$\begin{bmatrix} 2 & 3 & 2 & 1 \\ 1 & 2 & 3.5 & 2 \\ 2 & 0.5 & 2 & 3 \\ 3 & 2 & 1 & 2 \end{bmatrix}.$$
>
> When using the simplex method to determine an optimal column strategy, does the strategy change when using different allowable pivots?

Chapter 9

Markov Chains

In this chapter, we will use the fact that spreadsheets are very efficient at computing powers, products, and inverses of matrices to allow us to gain a better understanding of using Markov chain models with large, real world sets of data. The *Excel* commands used in this section include MMULT and MINVERSE which were introduced in chapter 2. One other tool we will use is a visual basic function we have created called MATRIXPOWER which computes powers of a given matrix.[1]

9.1 S&P Bond Ratings

[Download: BondsProject.xls]

Standard and Poor's uses different ratings in evaluating bond risk. These ratings (AAA, AA, A, BBB, BB, B, CCC) range from little risk (AAA) to high risk (CCC). The transition matrix shown in Figure 9.1 shows the probability of each type of bond changing catagories or defaulting during a given year.[2] Each entry in a row shows the probability that a bond with a rating shown in the first column ends up one year later in the category shown in the column headings. For example, the probability that a BB bond will be upgraded to an A bond after one year is 0.61%.

The federal government is considering investing part of the Social Security trust fund in bonds. Being averse to risk, the government will originally invest only in 50% AAA bonds, 25% AA bonds, and 25% A bonds. Assuming these bonds all have 30 years to maturity, one of our goals will be to predict how many years are likely to pass before 0.5% of these bonds are in default. We would also like to determine a bond investment strategy which will both a) maximize the government's return (the

---

[1] Source code for this visual basic function is included in the appendix of this chapter for the interested reader.

[2] Average annual transition matrix for years 1981-1998.

CHAPTER 9. MARKOV CHAINS

higher the risk on a bond, the higher the return) and b) keep the percentage of bonds the government owns that are in default to under 0.5%.

	AAA	AA	A	BBB	BB	B	CCC	Default
AAA	91.93%	7.46%	0.48%	0.08%	0.04%	0.00%	0.00%	0.00%
AA	0.64%	91.82%	6.77%	0.62%	0.08%	0.06%	0.01%	0.00%
A	0.07%	2.27%	91.65%	5.12%	0.56%	0.25%	0.03%	0.04%
BBB	0.04%	0.27%	5.56%	87.89%	4.83%	1.02%	0.17%	0.22%
BB	0.04%	0.10%	0.61%	7.76%	81.55%	7.90%	1.11%	0.92%
B	0.00%	0.10%	0.43%	0.81%	7.00%	82.86%	3.99%	4.82%
CCC	0.00%	0.04%	0.28%	0.47%	2.57%	12.69%	63.56%	20.39%
Default	0.00%	0.00%	0.00%	0.00%	0.00%	0.00%	0.00%	100.00%

Figure 9.1: S&P's bond rating transition matrix.

1. According to Figure 9.1, what is the probability that a BBB bond will be in default after one year? What is the probability that a BBB bond will be upgraded to an A bond after one year?

2. Suppose you initially invest in 100% AAA bonds. Using the spreadsheet 'S&P Bond Ratings,' determine the percentage of bonds that you own after one year that will most likely be in default? after two years? after 15 years?[3]

3. If you initially invest 100% in AAA bonds, estimate how many years would likely pass before at least 0.2% of your bonds were in default?

4. If you initially invest 50% in CCC bonds and 50% in BB bonds (because they yield a higher rate of return), what percentage of the bonds you invested in will be in default after one year? after two years? after 15 years?

5. The federal government is considering investing part of the Social Security trust fund in bonds. Being averse to risk, the government will originally invest only in 50% AAA bonds, 25% AA bonds, and 25% A bonds. Assuming these bonds all have 30 years to maturity, decide how many years are likely to pass before 0.5% of these bonds are in default. If the government were to 'clean house' and sell all bonds rated below A at this point, what percentage of the investments would need to be sold?

6. Interpret the entry $F_{7,7}$ found in the **fundamental matrix** F computed in the spreadsheet 'S&P Bond Ratings.'

---

[3] We assume, for the sake of simplicity, that the time until these bonds mature is longer than 15 years.

7. Label the S&P bond rating transition matrix of Figure 9.1 as P. Explain why the limiting matrix $\overline{P}$ has no meaningful interpretation in this problem.

> **You make the call:** Discuss possible investment strategies the government could use which would meet their goal of a) maximizing return and b) limiting the number of bonds in default in their portfolio in any given year to 0.5%.

9.2 Raising Neptunian Iguanas

[Download: GeneticsProject.xls]

The latest pet craze to sweep the nation has been that of the blue-eyed Neptunian iguana. The gene in the Neptunian iguanas which gives blue eyes is recessive. Neptunian iguanas having brown eyes possess the dominant gene. To be more precise, an iguana having blue eyes has gene type bb; an iguana having brown eyes either has gene type Bb or BB. That is, a brown-eyed iguana could have one dominant 'B' gene and also be a carrier of the recessive blue-eyed gene 'b.'

Imagine you own a Neptunian iguana breeding farm in which you start with two iguanas of opposite sex, mate them, select two of their offspring of opposite sex, and mate those, and so forth. There are six different states in which a pair of mating iguanas could belong: s_1=(BB,BB), s_2=(BB,Bb), s_3=(BB,bb), s_4=(Bb,Bb), s_5=(Bb,bb), and s_6=(bb,bb).

Each parent will give one of its genes, B or b, to an offspring with equal probability. For example, suppose the male parent has BB genes and the female parent has Bb genes. Then, the probability of having a BB offspring is 0.5. The probability of having a Bb offspring is 0.5. Of course, we will force each set of parents on our iguana farm to have exactly one pair of offspring. In this case, the probability of having an offspring pair in state s_1=(BB,BB) is 0.25. The probability of having an offspring pair in state s_2=(BB,Bb) is 0.5 and the probability of having an offspring pair in state s_4=(Bb,Bb) is 0.25. Notice how it is impossible for this set of parents of have an offspring pair in state s_3=(BB,bb) since the male parent cannot give an offspring a 'b' gene.

A transition matrix describing this mating process is shown in Figure 9.2. This matrix shows, for example, that the probability of a male and female pair of brown-eyed carriers (state s_4=(Bb,Bb)) having a pair of blue-eyed offspring (state s_6=(bb,bb)) is 0.0625.

Our goal in this project is to use the given transition matrix data to develop a strategy for operating a Neptunian iguana breeding farm.

	Bb,bb	BB,Bb	BB,bb	Bb,Bb	BB,BB	bb,bb
Bb,bb	0.5	0	0	0.25	0	0.25
BB,Bb	0	0.5	0	0.25	0.25	0
BB,bb	0	0	0	1	0	0
Bb,Bb	0.25	0.25	0.125	0.25	0.0625	0.0625
BB,BB	0	0	0	0	1	0
bb,bb	0	0	0	0	0	1

Figure 9.2: Transition matrix for the Neptunian iguana farm.

CHAPTER 9. MARKOV CHAINS

1. According to Figure 9.2, what is the probability that a set of parents in state s_4=(Bb,Bb) will have a pair of offspring in state s_5=(Bb,bb)? What is the probability that a set of parents in state s_4=(Bb,Bb) will have a blue-eyed offspring?

2. Assume you begin your Neptunian iguana farm with 100 pairs of (Bb,Bb) iguanas (all brown-eyed!). Furthermore, we will assume that we sell each of these parents after they have offspring (so that our farm will always have 100 pairs of iguanas). Using the spreadsheet 'Neptunian Iguana Farm,' estimate how many pairs of blue-eyed iguanas you should expect to have after one mating season. How many pairs of blue-eyed iguanas should you expect to have after two mating seasons? after three seasons?

3. Again assume you begin your Neptunian iguana farm with 100 pairs of (Bb,Bb) iguanas and that we sell each of these parents after they have offspring. Estimate the number of mating seasons required before we should expect to have 45 blue-eyed iguanas on our farm at which time the farm becomes profitable.

4. What kinds of eye color traits should we expect our iguana farm to have after a large number of mating seasons? Decide whether or not we should keep any brown-eyed iguanas on the farm at that point in the hope that they might produce blue-eyed iguanas. Would it be wise to reduce the size of the farm to 50 pairs of iguanas? Explain.

5. Let us assume now that the iguana farm begins with 100 pairs of (BB,Bb) iguanas and that, once again, we sell each of the parents after they have a pair of offspring. Estimate how many pairs of blue-eyed iguanas you should expect to have after one mating season. How many pairs of blue-eyed iguanas should you expect to have after two mating seasons? after 10 seasons? after 100 seasons? Develop a strategy for managing this iguana farm effectively. That is, how and when might you reduce the size of the farm so as to not have to care for so many useless brown-eyed iguanas?

6. Assuming brown-eyed iguanas have a value of zero, but blue-eyed iguanas have a value of $100 each, which scenario would lead to the most profit: a farm beginning with 100 pairs of (Bb,Bb) iguanas or a farm beginning with 100 pairs of (BB,Bb) iguanas? How much more profit per generation would this farm yield in the long run?

7. Suppose we were to start an iguana farm with 20 pairs each in states s_1 through s_5; that is, an initial state of (20,20,20,20,20,0). Compare the profit per generation this farm would yield in the long run to the previous two farms considered.

CHAPTER 9. MARKOV CHAINS

8. Assume the transition matrix P has the block form

$$\begin{bmatrix} Q & R \\ 0 & I \end{bmatrix}$$

so that the fundamental matrix F is given by $F = (I - Q)^{-1}$. From the spreadsheet 'Neptunian Iguana Farm,' we see that the entries of the first two rows of the fundamental matrix F both sum to 4.83333. What does this number represent? Does this number make sense? Explain.

9. Interpret the (1,2) entry of the matrix FR given in the spreadsheet. Explain why the entries of FR in this example all seem reasonable.

> **You make the call:** If it costs \$2 for a BB iguana, \$8 for a Bb iguana, and \$100 for a bb (blue-eyed) iguana, discuss how it is that we should initially stock our iguana farm. How should the farm be managed from mating season to mating season to optimize profit?

9.3 Tennis Anyone?

[Download: TennisProject.xls]

When professional tennis players Andre Agassi and Pete Sampras play each other, the score of a game is often tied at deuce. Assuming for the moment that the having the serve is not a big advantage,[4] we can use the past history between the two players, Markov chains, and a spreadsheet to determine how long we can expect to wait on average for the game to be completed and what the probability of each player winning will be.

Consider, in general, the game of tennis when the score of *deuce* is reached. If one player wins the next point, they are said to have the *advantage*. On the following point, they either win the game or the game returns to the score of deuce. We will assume, for the sake of argument, that player A has a probability p of winning any given point and player B has probability $1 - p$ of winning any given point.

1. Set up a transition matrix for this process in which we consider five states: s_1=player A wins, s_2=player B wins, s_3=advantage A, s_4=advantage B, and s_5=deuce.

2. If player A has a 60% chance of winning any given point, use the spreadsheet 'Tennis Transitions' to compute the probability that player A will win the game after two points are played. What is the probability that player A will win the game after three points are played? after four points?

3. If player A has a 60% chance of winning any given point, what is the probability that the game will not be over after two points have been played? After how many points is the chance that the game will be over greater than 95%?

4. What is the probability that the game will again be at deuce after 3 points have been played? after 5 points? after 7 points? Can you draw any conclusions? Did you really need to do any calculations?

5. How "good" must player A be in order to win 90% of all the games tied at deuce in the long run?

6. If the game starts at an advantage for player B, how "good" must player A be in order to have a 50-50 chance of eventually winning the game?

---

[4]Having the serve really IS a big advantage. However, the same general study can be done when the service advantage is considered.

CHAPTER 9. MARKOV CHAINS 162

7. Assume the transition matrix P has the block form

$$\begin{bmatrix} Q & R \\ 0 & I \end{bmatrix}$$

so that the fundamental matrix F is given by $F = (I - Q)^{-1}$. Using the matrix F computed by the spreadsheet 'Tennis Transitions,' determine how long you should expect a game between two evenly matched players to last if the game is at deuce. How long do you expect a game starting at deuce to last (on average) if player A has an 80% chance of winning any given point?

8. Interpret the (2,2) entry of the matrix FR calculated in the spreadsheet 'Tennis Transitions.' Compare the value of this entry with the final state matrix when $N = 100$ and the initial state of the game is (0,1,0,0,0). Can you draw any conclusions?

> **You make the call:** When meeting on grass surfaces, Pete Sampras has about a 57% chance of winning any given point when matched against Andre Agassi. Estimate the probability that on grass, when the game is at deuce, Sampras will win the game. How long should a game at deuce between the players be expected to last?

CHAPTER 9. MARKOV CHAINS

9.4 Game, Set, Math!

[Download: AnotherTennisProject.xls]

When meeting on grass surfaces, professional tennis player Pete Sampras has won 43 games to his rival Andre Agassi's 32. With the use of a Markov chain, we can estimate the probability that on grass, Agassi will win any given point when matched up with Sampras. Further, and perhaps useful to the major TV networks, we can estimate how long we should expect a given game between the two competitors to last.

To the uninitiated, a game of tennis has a strange scoring system. Possible scores include love/love, 30/15, 40/love, deuce, and advantage. Despite the strange nomenclature, scoring is quite easy to understand. To win a single game of tennis requires the scoring of four points and it requires that one win by a margin of two points.

With this, an entire game of tennis can be considered to be a Markov process. In such a process there are 20 possible states - one for each possible score of the game. In this process, by having the second player score, a score of 3-3 (deuce) is attainable from a score of 4-3. When the first player wins a point, a score of 3-3 is also attainable from a score of 3-4. A 20 × 20 transition matrix modeling a single game in which the probability of each player winning any given point is input can be found in the workbook `AnotherTennisProject.xls`.

1. Suppose two tennis players are evenly matched. Use the spreadsheet 'Game, Set, Math!' to determine the most likely outcome after four points have been played. after five points? It may seem that 3-3 (deuce) is the most likely score after six points have been played. Is that the case?

2. If one tennis player is likely to win 51% of the points in a given game, what is the probability of that player winning the game? Given that a game is tied at 2-2, what is the probability that this player will win the game? If a game is tied at 3-3 (deuce), what is the probability that this player will win the game? Can you explain the differences in the outcomes coming from a 2-2 tie and a 3-3 tie?

3. In order to have a 90% chance of winning any given game, what is the smallest advantage a player can have over their opponent on any given point? That is, how likely must it be for a player to win any given point? *Hint:* If a player has a 90% chance of winning any given *point*, they have a whopping 99.86% chance of winning any given *game*!

4. In head to head competition, Pete Sampras leads Andre Agassi 17 matches to 12 matches. However, Agassi has won 399 games to Sampras' 394 in head to

CHAPTER 9. MARKOV CHAINS 164

head matchups.[5] Based on the fact that Agassi has a 50.32% probability of winning a given game between the two, use the spreadsheet 'Game, Set, Math!' to estimate the probability that Agassi can win any given point when matched up with Sampras.

5. Assume the transition matrix P has the block form

$$\begin{bmatrix} Q & R \\ 0 & I \end{bmatrix}$$

so that the fundamental matrix F is given by $F = (I - Q)^{-1}$.

   (a) Using the matrix F computed by the spreadsheet 'Game, Set, Math!,' determine how long you should expect a game between two evenly matched players to last.

   (b) How many points longer do you expect a game already at a score of 0-2 to last (on average) if player A has an 80% chance of winning any given point?

6. Interpret the (3,2) entry of the matrix FR calculated in the spreadsheet. Compare the value of this entry with the final state matrix when $N = 100$ and the initial state of the game is set at a score of 0-1. Can you draw any conclusions?

> **You make the call:** When meeting on grass surfaces, Pete Sampras has won 43 games to Andre Agassi's 32. Use the spreadsheet 'Game, Set, Math!' to estimate the probability that on grass, Agassi will win any given point when matched up with Sampras. How long should a game on grass between the players be expected to last?

---

[5]Source: onlinesql.itftennis.com

9.5 Tumblin' Gumballs

[Download: GumballsProject.xls]

Just like tennis, many other games can be modeled using Markov chains. We now model the Fisher-Price game called *Tumblin' Gumballs*. We will make some assumptions in order to simplify the Markov chain used in modeling the game. We assume that we have two players - they will have three blue (B) and three red (R) gumballs respectively. The gumball machine will contain two different colors of gumballs - green (G), and yellow (Y). On each turn a player will put a gumball into the gumball machine, turn the handle of the machine, and take a (possible different) gumball out of the machine. This process continues until one player has three different colored gumballs and is declared the winner.

Figure 9.3: The Tumblin' Gumballs game by Fisher-Price.

This particular game has 23 possible states; six in which the blue player is the winner and six in which the red player is the winner. There are two transition matrices we need to consider in this problem. There is a transition matrix P_1 for the blue player's turn and a transition matrix P_2 for the red player's turn. If we start in state matrix S, then the state of the game after the blue player starts the game is given by SP_1. The state matrix of the game after both player's have a turn is SP_1P_2. Immediately after the blue player P_1 takes his 14th turn, the state matrix for the game is given by $S(P_1P_2)^{13}P_1$.

Our goal for this project is to analyze the probability of each player winning the game and how long we should expect the game to take.

CHAPTER 9. MARKOV CHAINS

1. According to the transition matrix given in the spreadsheet 'Tumblin' Gumballs,' what is the probability of moving from state BBY GR RRB to state BGY BR RRB during the blue player's turn? What is the probability of moving from state BBY GR RRB to state BBY GR RRB during the red player's turn?

2. What is the probability of having a winner after two turns have been taken by the blue player P_1 and one turn has been taken by the red player P_2? What are the two most likely states given that the blue player has won after these turns?

3. After each player takes three turns, what is the probability that the red player P_2 has won? If the red player does win after three turns, what is the least likely state the game will be in?

4. Suppose that it has occurred that the blue player P_1 took its first turn and received a blue chip upon play and that the red player took a turn and received a yellow chip on its first play. What is the probability that the red player will eventually win this game?

5. Assume the joint transition matrix $P_1 P_2$ has the block form

$$\begin{bmatrix} Q & R \\ 0 & I \end{bmatrix}$$

so that the fundamental matrix F is given by $F = (I - Q)^{-1}$. Interpret the meaning of the sum of the elements in the first row of F (2.95 in our example). Does it make sense that the sums of all the other rows of F are smaller than the sum of the first row? Explain.

6. Interpret the (1,2) entry of the matrix FR. Explain why it is perfectly logical for the (4,1) entry of FR to be 0.

7. By taking 100 turns, determine the probability that the blue player P_1 will eventually win this game. Without taking any turns, what information on the spreadsheet could you put together to compute this probability? How long do you expect this game to take?

> **You make the call:** In Tumblin' Gumballs, the youngest player is always the blue player P_1. If you were to play 9 games of Tumblin' Gumballs with your four year old niece, use the spreadsheet 'Tumblin' Gumballs' to determine how many games you should expect to win. How much time should you budget to play 9 games?

9.6 Juvenile Recidivism in New South Wales

[Download: JuvenileProject.xls]

A 1999 study on juvenile recidivism in New South Wales[6] produced a table as shown in Figure 9.4 containing the probabilities that a juvenile who has a proven court appearance for a specific offense on one occasion will have a proven court appearance for the same or any other offense on a subsequent occasion.

	Violent Offense	Robbery	Break & Enter	Vehicle Theft	Other Theft	Drug Offense	Other Offenses
Violent Offense	28.3%	2.9%	11.7%	6.0%	13.5%	4.0%	33.7%
Robbery	18.2%	7.7%	10.2%	11.6%	12.9%	3.4%	36.1%
Break & Enter	14.0%	2.3%	26.3%	6.4%	17.8%	3.6%	29.6%
Vehicle Theft	14.8%	2.2%	12.0%	19.5%	15.3%	6.1%	30.2%
Other Theft	16.3%	2.8%	13.5%	8.9%	25.9%	4.0%	28.5%
Drug Offenses	11.3%	2.4%	13.0%	6.0%	16.4%	17.0%	34.0%
Other Offenses	18.7%	2.4%	13.0%	7.8%	17.2%	4.9%	36.1%

Figure 9.4: Transition matrix depicting juvenile recidivism in New South Wales.

This matrix shows, for example, that among offenders recording a proven court appearance for robbery, there is an 18.2% chance of a subsequent proven court appearance for violent offenses such as assault or homicide.

1. According to Figure 9.4, what is the probability that a juvenile with a proven court appearance for vehicle theft will have a subsequent proven court appearance for vehicle theft? What is the probability that a juvenile with a proven court appearance for a drug offense will have a subsequent proven court appearance for a violent offense?

2. Using the spreadsheet 'Juvenile Offenses,' determine if the transition matrix P is regular.

3. Using the spreadsheet 'Juvenile Offenses' containing the transition matrix P, estimate the limiting matrix $\overline{P}$.

> **You make the call:** From the limiting matrix $\overline{P}$ found using the spreadsheet 'Juvenile Offenses,' determine the steady state matrix S for this Markov process. What does this steady state matrix S represent in terms of juvenile recidivism in New South Wales?

---

[6]Source: "Recidivism and the Juvenile Offender", Carlos Carcach, Australian Institute of Criminology.

9.7 Appendix

Source code for the visual basic function `MATRIXPOWER`:

```
Function matrixpower(matrix, n)
   If n = 1 Then
      matrixpower = matrix
      Else:  matrixpower = Application.MMult(matrixpower(matrix, n - 1), matrix)
   End If
End Function
```

Index

ADD TRENDLINE, 12
AVERAGE, 137, 138
BINOMDIST, 108
CHART, 12
COMBIN, 115
COUNTIF, 131, 134, 138, 139
CRITBINOM, 114
CRTL, 29
Chart Wizard, 27, 29
Chart, 27
Data, 129, 133, 139
FALSE, 124
FV, 92
Format Axis, 28
Format, 131
Forms, 138
Goal Seek, 19--21, 23, 92, 95, 97, 98, 100, 124, 125, 128
HYPGEOMDIST, 120, 121
INDEX, 138
Insert, 27
LINEAR, 12
MAX, 138, 140
MDETERM, 49
MEDIAN, 138
MINVERSE, 36, 41, 51
MIN, 138, 140
MMULT, 32, 41, 51, 69, 148
MODE, 138
NEGBINOMDIST, 111
NORMDIST, 123, 124, 127
OPTIONS, 12
PERCENTILE, 138, 140, 141

PERCENTRANK, 138, 142
PMT, 92, 102
PV, 93
ROUNDUP, 115
SCATTER PLOT, 12
SQRT, 6, 64, 127
STDEVP, 142
STDEV, 142
SUMPRODUCT, 108
SUM, 3, 66, 127, 132, 152
Scale, 28
Scatter Plot, 27, 130
Series, 29
Solver Parameters, 55, 60
Solver, 53, 55, 60, 62--69, 72, 96, 153
Sort, 129, 133, 139
TRANSPOSE, 47
TRUE, 124
Tools, 20, 25, 53, 55, 60, 64, 66, 69, 72, 95, 124, 128, 153